DRYWALL
PROFESSIONAL TECHNIQUES FOR WALLS & CEILINGS

DRYWALL
PROFESSIONAL TECHNIQUES FOR WALLS & CEILINGS

MYRON R. FERGUSON

The Taunton Press

COVER PHOTO: SUSAN KAHN

Taunton
BOOKS & VIDEOS
for fellow enthusiasts

First printing: 1996

Printed in the United States of America

A Fine Homebuilding Book

Fine Homebuilding® is a trademark of The Taunton Press, Inc.,
registered in the U.S. Patent and Trademark Office.

The Taunton Press, 63 South Main Street, PO Box 5506,
Newtown, CT 06470-5506

Library of Congress Cataloging-in-Publication Data

Ferguson, Myron R.
    Drywall : professional techniques for walls & ceilings / Myron R. Ferguson.
        p.   cm.
    Includes index.
    ISBN 1-56158-133-X (pbk.)
    1. Dry wall.   I. Title.
TH2239.F47   1996
690'.12 — dc20   96-21908
                                                  CIP

To Linda, my wife and best friend

ACKNOWLEDGMENTS

Most of what I've learned during my 16 years in the drywall trade has been through trial and error and researching and using new products and tools. In the early days, I often wished there was a guide on how to work with drywall from start to finish, but there was no one book that presented the information in a straightforward, easy-to-understand manner. This is the book I was looking for, and I hope it will serve you as an invaluable guide, whether you're a beginner getting ready to hang your very first drywall panel or a pro searching for tips on the latest techniques and materials.

For helping to make this book possible, I'd like to thank all the folks at The Taunton Press who've worked with me, especially Julie Trelstad, for giving me the opportunity to write this book, and Peter Chapman, for shaping my words and ideas into something so easy to understand. Thanks also to Richard Duncan, whose work on my proposal for this book helped me get my foot in the door in the first place, and to the United States Gypsum Company, Georgia Pacific and the National Gypsum Company for all the information on drywall they sent me.

Many thanks to my photographer, Jay Holz, who was there when I was just thinking about writing a book and stuck with me till the end, always positive and offering encouragement as he followed me from job to job, even with his busy schedule. I'm also grateful to all the people who let me use their homes or equipment for the photo shoots. And I must thank Jeff Wagoner and Ira Cromling, the subcontractors who work for me (you'll see them both in photos throughout the book). I know there were many times when I left them with all the work when I had to get ready for photos, talk to my editor or do one of the many other tasks that have to happen to make a book possible.

And finally, a huge thanks to my wife, Linda, who worked with me many late nights and weekends, doing all the computer work, offering editorial suggestions and keeping me on schedule. I couldn't have done the book without her.

CONTENTS

INTRODUCTION

Drywall, wallboard, Sheetrock, gypsum board...call it what you will, this material is on more walls and ceilings than any other material in new construction. Properly installed, drywall can add real beauty to a home or business. Improperly attached, it can be a major eyesore. In this book, I'll teach you how to do it right, with techniques and materials used by the pros.

My first drywalling job was on my own house several years ago. I'd heard a lot of negative things about the chore of installing drywall, but to my surprise I found that I liked the work. Hanging the panels provided me with the physical work that I enjoy, while taping and finishing the drywall proved to be an interesting test of my patience and skill. When I started out in the business in 1980, I had a bare minimum of tools and a pretty limited knowledge of the drywall trade. But over the years, I've experimented with different kinds of drywall, joint tape and joint compounds, added numerous tools to my drywalling arsenal and studied the work of several professional hangers and tapers. All that, combined with countless hours spent hanging and taping drywall, has enabled me to develop techniques that virtually guarantee success when drywalling.

If you've ever watched a professional hanger or taper in action, the work probably looked deceptively simple—panels are attached and joints taped in a graceful rhythm. But don't be deceived, working with drywall is not without its frustrations. Getting the perfect finish on the final coat of joint compound can be maddening, and finding a highly conspicuous ridge running the length of the ceiling after you've painted can all but reduce you to tears. Drywalling requires care and attention to detail at every step of the way—and knowing when to use one type of drywall rather than another, screws rather than nails, mesh rather than paper tape, and drying-type compound rather than setting-type compound.

Drywalling is a very linear process, and I've organized the book in roughly the order I handle a typical job—from planning the layout, hanging, taping and sanding the drywall, to finishing the walls and ceiling (with paint, textures or wall coverings). I've also included a chapter on special installations (such as curved walls and double-layer applications) and another on drywall repairs. It's a complete course in drywalling.

DRYWALL BASICS

During the 1940s and 1950s prefabricated drywall panels gradually replaced plaster as the material of choice for finishing interior walls and ceilings. The earliest drywall panels were used to replace the lath backing in plaster work; they were narrow (16 in. wide) and only ³⁄₈ in. thick. Today, drywall comes in a wide variety of lengths, thicknesses and special-use panels. The low material cost and the large, easy-to-attach panels combine to make drywall the popular choice over conventional plaster.

Plaster-and-lath construction added a lot of moisture to the building, and plastered surfaces had to be left to dry for up to two weeks (depending on humidity, temperature and airflow) before decorating. By comparison, drywall has a low moisture content and the joint compounds used to finish the panels cover only a portion of the surface, not the entire surface, and dry in 24 hours or less. Hence the name *dry*wall (drywall is known by many other names as well, such as Sheetrock—a brand name, gypsum board, plasterboard, wallboard and gypsum drywall).

A sheet of drywall consists of a hardened gypsum core sandwiched between two layers of paper: a strong, smooth finished paper on one side (the face), and a rougher, "natural" paper on the back (see the drawing on the facing page). The face paper is folded around the long edges, which are tapered slightly to accommodate joint tape and compound after the panel is installed. The ends of the panel are cut square and finished smooth, with the gypsum core exposed.

TYPES AND USES OF DRYWALL

When most people think of drywall, they probably picture the standard 4x8 panel that's been in use since drywall first became popular. But this is by no means the only size or type of drywall available today. Panels come in lengths up to 16 ft., in 48-in. and 54-in. widths and in a wide variety of special-use panels, including moisture-resistant, fire-resistant and abuse-resistant panels, ¼-in. flexible panels, ½-in. high-strength ceiling panels, and foil-backed panels. In this section, I'll guide you through the various types, their uses, the thicknesses and lengths available and the framing specifications for each type. With this information, you'll be able to make the right decision about what type of drywall to order when it comes time to plan the job.

Regular drywall

Regular drywall panels are 48 in. wide and come in a variety of lengths from 8 ft. to 16 ft. (see the chart below). Panels are available in four thicknesses (5⁄8 in., 1⁄2 in., 3⁄8 in. and 1⁄4 in.), each with specific applications (and framing requirements).

Five-eighth-inch regular drywall

Five-eighth-inch drywall is the thickest regular drywall available and provides the best single-layer application on walls and ceilings over wood and metal framing. The panels provide greater resistance to fire and deaden sound better than the other thicknesses; and because the panels are stiffer, they are more resistant to sagging. Five-eighth-inch drywall can be used on walls and ceilings with framing members (wall studs and ceiling joists) spaced up to 24 in. on center (o.c.). If you install (or

END VIEW OF A DRYWALL PANEL

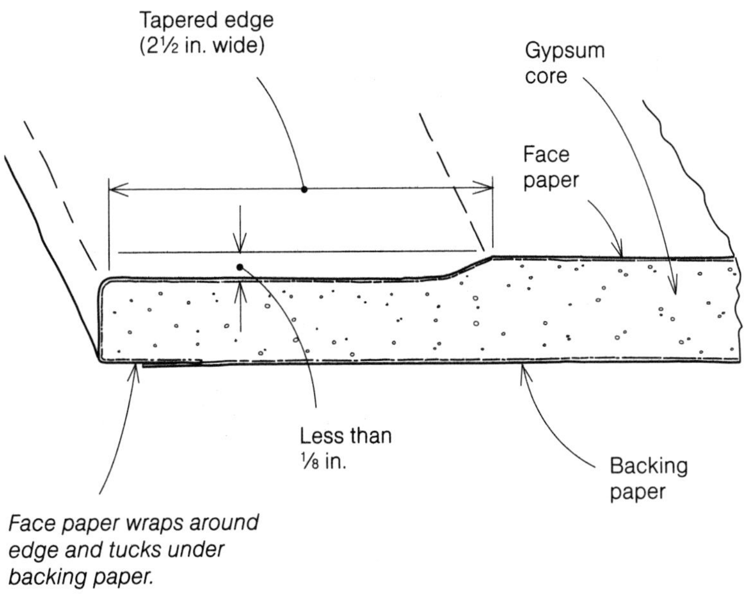
Tapered edge
(2½ in. wide)
Gypsum
core
Face
paper
Less than
⅛ in.
Backing
paper
Face paper wraps around
edge and tucks under
backing paper.

REGULAR DRYWALL

Thickness	Common Uses	Available Lengths	Maximum Framing Spacing
5⁄8 in.	Walls and ceilings	8 ft., 9 ft., 10 ft., 12 ft., 14 ft.	24 in. o.c.; 16 in. o.c. if textured or hung parallel to ceiling joists
1⁄2 in.	Walls and ceilings (most common type of drywall used)	8 ft., 9 ft., 10 ft., 12 ft., 14 ft., 16 ft.	24 in. o.c.; 16 in. o.c. if textured or hung parallel to ceiling joists
3⁄8 in.	Remodeling, mainly on walls	8 ft., 10 ft., 12 ft.	16 in. o.c.
1⁄4 in.	Remodeling over solid surfaces or curved surfaces with long radii	8 ft., 10 ft.	16 in. o.c. as double layer or as single layer over solid surface

"hang") the panels parallel to ceiling joists, the joists should be no farther apart than 16 in. o.c. to prevent sagging. If you hang ⅝-in. panels perpendicular to ceiling joists, a water-based texture can be applied only if the ceiling joists are 16 in. o.c. or closer (again, to avoid sagging).

Half-inch regular drywall Half-inch drywall is the most commonly used drywall in both new construction and remodeling. It is usually used as a single layer over wood or metal framing, but it can be installed in two layers (with staggered seams) to increase fire resistance and sound control. The framing requirements for ½-in. drywall are the same as for ⅝-in. panels. If the framing is farther apart than the recommended spacing, wood or metal furring strips can be attached across the framing to the specified on-center spacing.

Three-eighth-inch regular drywall
Three-eighth-inch drywall was initially used to replace wood lath as a backing for plaster. When drywall first became popular, ⅜ in. was widely used on walls and ceilings in new construction, but it was eventually replaced by the more durable ½-in. drywall. Today, ⅜-in. drywall is used mainly in repair and remodeling work to cover existing surfaces or as a backing for paneling. It is also used in double-layer applications. The maximum distance between framing members on walls and ceilings is 16 in. o.c. For installation on studs and joists that are more than 16 in. o.c. apart, use a double layer of ⅜-in. drywall with adhesive applied between the two layers (see p. 105).

Quarter-inch regular drywall Quarter-inch drywall is a lightweight panel that is used to cover old walls and ceiling surfaces in remodeling jobs or for sound control in double-layer or multilayer applications. When hanging ¼-in. drywall over old plaster or drywall, adhesive is used between the old surface and the new drywall in combination with screws to help strengthen the panels and reduce sag. The thin panels are too weak to install in a single layer over bare studs or joists without backing. Regular ¼-in. drywall is easily bent and can be used to form curved surfaces with long radii (5 ft. or more) if applied dry, or shorter radii (3 ft. or more) if applied wet. A better choice for curved surfaces, however, is ¼-in. flexible drywall, which is discussed later in this chapter. Maximum on-center framing for ¼-in. regular drywall is 16 in. (either as a double layer or as a single layer over an existing solid surface).

Moisture-resistant drywall

Moisture-resistant drywall, which has a light-green or blue face paper to distinguish it from other types of drywall (hence the name greenboard or blueboard), is designed to minimize moisture problems. The panels, which are moisture-resistant all the way through, are made to withstand high humidity and low levels of moisture. Moisture-resistant drywall is used mainly in bathrooms, and to cover the bottom 4 ft. of a laundry or utility room or the wall behind a kitchen sink. It is an excellent base for ceramic, plastic or metal tile applied with an adhesive, or for other nonabsorbent finishes such as paint, wallpaper or plastic tub surrounds.

Moisture-resistant drywall should not be used in wet or high-moisture areas, or in areas exposed to constant moisture. If used on the lower portion of a tub wall or on a shower enclosure, it should be covered with a tub surround or tile. In addition, it should not be hung over a plastic vapor barrier or a painted wall: Moisture-resistant drywall should be attached directly to the framing to avoid creating a double vapor barrier, which would eventually deteriorate the drywall if any moisture were to get in. In areas that are not covered with tile or other

MOISTURE-RESISTANT DRYWALL

Thickness	Common Uses	Available Lengths	Maximum Framing Spacing
½ in.	Bathrooms, damp areas	8 ft., 10 ft., 12 ft. (up to 16 ft. as special order)	16 in. o.c. on walls; 12 in. o.c. on ceilings
⅝ in.	Bathroom ceilings; fire walls in damp or high-humidity areas	8 ft., 10 ft., 12 ft. (up to 16 ft. as special order)	16 in. o.c. on walls; 12 in. o.c. on ceilings

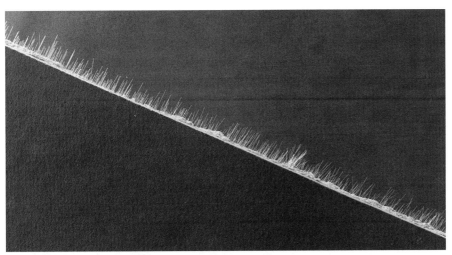

Fire-resistant drywall panels have a gypsum core with glass fibers that help contain fire.

wall coverings, moisture-resistant drywall can be taped and painted the same as any other type of drywall.

Moisture-resistant drywall, which is available in ½-in. regular or ⅝-in. fire resistant, is used mainly as a wall covering over 16-in. o.c. framing. If you plan to install it on a ceiling, use ⅝ in. over 16-in. centers and ½ in. over 12-in. (or less) centers. (If the ceiling is insulated, check to make sure that unfaced insulation was used to avoid creating a double vapor barrier.)

Fire-resistant drywall

As a dense material, drywall is a better barrier against fire (and a more efficient sound absorber) than lighter materials such as plywood, but one type of drywall is particularly effective in containing fire. Fire-resistant drywall panels have a gypsum core with special additives and glass fibers that aid in containing fire. On the surface, these panels look the same as regular drywall, except for a stamp that indicates that they are fire resistant. Fire-resistant drywall is a little harder to cut than regular drywall, because the gypsum core is tougher.

"Fire resistance" signifies the ability of a constructed assembly (the wall or ceiling that is covered with drywall) to contain a fire. The fire-resistance rating for each thickness of drywall is indicated with intervals of time: 45 minutes for ½-in. fire-resistant drywall, 60 minutes for ⅝ in. and 120 minutes for ¾ in. The panels can be layered to increase the fire rating.

Many building codes specify fire-resistant drywall for attached garages, for furnace or utility rooms, and for ceilings and walls separating dwelling units in apartment and condominium complexes. The two most commonly used fire-resistant panels are ½ in. and ⅝ in. Half-inch panels are convenient when you need to cover only part of a wall or ceiling with fire-resistant drywall and the rest with regular ½-in. drywall (the most common standard thickness). An example would be on a garage ceiling, where typically only the first 5 ft. of the ceiling adjacent to the house wall has to be fire resistant. Using matching thicknesses allows you to make a smooth transition at the joint. If you use different thicknesses (say, ⅝-in. fire resistant and ½-in. regular), you'll create a seam that's difficult to hide during the taping process.

Five-eighth-inch panels are the most commonly used fire-resistant panels. They provide the one-hour fire rating that many building codes require. Since most garage-ceiling joists are 24-in. o.c., ⅝-in. panels work best because they are approved for 24-in. spacing. Although manufacturers approve ½-in. panels for joists 24 in. o.c., these panels are more likely to sag, especially in a garage that is exposed to temperature and humidity extremes. Because of the extra thickness and stronger core, ⅝-in. fire resistant is a little more resistant than ½ in. to denting and other types of abuse. Since garages can come in for a lot of abuse from car doors, bikes and tools, I like to cover the entire surface with ⅝ in.

FIRE-RESISTANT DRYWALL

Thickness	Common Uses	Fire Rating	Available Lengths	Maximum Framing Spacing
½ in.	In areas where butted against regular ½ in.	45 min.	8 ft., 10 ft., 12 ft.	24 in. o.c.
⅝ in.	Garages and over 24-in. o.c. ceilings (most commonly used thickness)	60 min.	8 ft., 10 ft., 12 ft. (14 ft. as special order)	24 in. o.c.
¾ in.	Where high fire rating is required	120 min.	8 ft., 9 ft., 10 ft., 12 ft.	24 in. o.c.

Three-quarter-inch fire-resistant drywall has a two-hour fire rating, or a four-hour rating if double-layered. It is used where a high fire rating is a must, as between apartments or to separate offices from a garage or factory. The extra thickness and fire rating allow for fewer layers, cutting down on the cost of materials and labor.

Abuse-resistant drywall

Abuse-resistant drywall has a high-strength reinforced gypsum core sandwiched between a heavy paper on the face and a strong liner paper on the back. Available in ½-in. regular and ⅝-in. fire-resistant panels, this type of drywall resists dents and penetration from sharp objects and blunt impacts more effectively than regular ⅝-in. fire-resistant drywall (see the photo at right). It is also more resistant to cracking and warping.

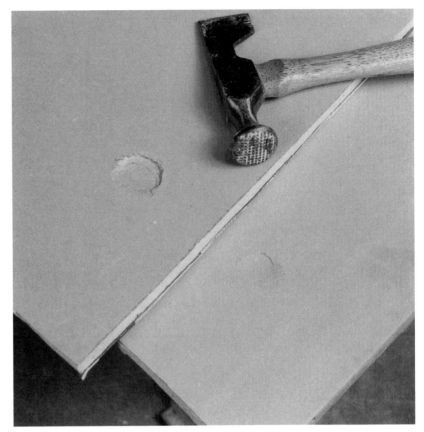

Abuse-resistant drywall (bottom panel) withstands heavy impact better than regular drywall (top).

ABUSE-RESISTANT DRYWALL			
Thickness	**Common Uses**	**Available Lengths**	**Maximum Framing Spacing**
½ in.	As an upgrade to regular drywall in high-traffic areas	8 ft., 10 ft., 12 ft.	24 in. o.c.
⅝ in.	As a fire wall in commercial and apartment buildings in high-traffic areas	8 ft., 10 ft., 12 ft.	24 in. o.c.

Half-inch abuse-resistant drywall is great for mudrooms, workshops and other high-traffic areas. The ⅝-in. panels are useful for commercial construction and apartment housing, since they provide the necessary fire protection and help to reduce maintenance costs.

Quarter-inch flexible drywall

Quarter-inch flexible drywall panels are designed for use on curved walls, archways and stairways. They work well on both concave and convex surfaces. Flexible drywall has a heavier face paper and a stronger liner paper than regular ¼-in. drywall and is more easily bent and more resistant to cracking caused by structural changes. It is usually applied in double layers, with staggered seams where possible.

Not all curved surfaces have the same radius—some are tighter than others. For curved surfaces with a short radius (32 in. or less), it may be necessary to wet the drywall before trying to attach it. Wetting the surface that will be compressed (with a sponge or roller) helps the drywall to form around the curve without breaking. (For more on this procedure, see Chapter 6.)

Flexible drywall panels are designed for use on archways and curved walls.

MINIMUM BENDING RADII OF ¼-IN. FLEXIBLE DRYWALL (ATTACHED LENGTHWISE)			
Type of Curve	**Wet or Dry**	**Minimum Radius**	**Maximum Stud Spacing**
Inside curve (concave)	Dry	32 in.	9 in. o.c.
Inside curve (concave)	Wet	20 in.	9 in. o.c.
Outside curve (convex)	Dry	32 in.	9 in. o.c.
Outside curve (convex)	Wet	15 in.	6 in. o.c.

Half-inch high-strength ceiling panels

Half-inch high-strength ceiling panels have a reinforced gypsum core that increases resistance to sagging, a common problem when using regular 1/2-in. drywall on widely spaced framing, or when applying water-based textures over drywall. High-strength drywall is rigid enough to hang over 24-in. o.c. joists (rather than 16 in. o.c., as I recommend for regular 1/2-in. drywall) and can be textured without fear of sagging. Half-inch high strength is available in lengths of 8 ft. and 12 ft. (lengths up to 16 ft. can be special-ordered).

Foil-backed drywall

Foil-backed drywall has aluminum foil laminated to the back of the panel. The foil creates an effective vapor barrier, as well as adding to the insulating value of the drywall. It is used mainly in cold climates to help prevent interior moisture from entering wall or ceiling cavities.

Foil-backed drywall can be used over wood and metal framing, over furred masonry, or as the base layer for multi-layer applications. It should not be used as a base for tile or highly moisture-resistant wall coverings, such as vinyl wallpaper, since the core could absorb and trap some moisture and eventually damage the drywall. Foil-backed drywall is also not recommended for use in hot, humid climates. Panels are available in 3/8-in., 1/2-in. and 5/8-in. thicknesses in the same lengths as for regular drywall.

54-in. wide drywall

One of the main aims when hanging drywall is to have as few seams as possible. That's fine when hanging 4-ft. wide sheets on walls with 8-ft. (or lower) ceilings—panels can be hung horizontally with just one seam (see p. 12 for an explanation of why I prefer to hang drywall horizontally, rather than vertically). But more and more homes are being constructed with 9-ft. ceilings, which means that with 4-ft. wide drywall you'd need two horizontal seams on each wall.

The way to avoid the extra seam is to use 54-in. drywall panels, which were introduced in the early 1990s for use on 9-ft. ceilings. Fifty-four-inch drywall comes in regular 1/2-in. or 5/8-in. fire-resistant panels. Sheets are readily available in 12-ft. lengths, but special lengths from 8 ft. to 16 ft. can be ordered. Fifty-four-inch drywall has the same framing specifications as regular 4-ft. wide panels.

WHY USE DRYWALL?

Regardless of type, all drywall panels have common characteristics that make them more suitable for use as wall coverings than plaster, plywood and other materials.

• Panels are available at most lumber stores in a variety of lengths.

• Panels are easy to cut and install.

• When properly reinforced with tape and joint compound, drywall panels are highly resistant to cracks.

• Panels readily accept paint and most other decorating materials.

• Drywall eliminates excessive moisture during construction—a problem with plaster applications.

• The noncombustible gypsum core provides fire protection.

• The dense panels provide more effective sound control than lighter materials such as plywood and fiberboard.

Cement board, which has one side smooth and one side rough, is used primarily as an underlayment for tile in areas exposed to water.

Gypsum-core tile backer, which is used as an underlayment for tile, has a silicone-treated core sandwiched between a layer of glass mat on either side. The face of the panel has an acrylic coating.

Cement board

Cement board is designed for use in areas exposed to water or high levels of moisture. This type of board is an excellent base for tile on walls and floors and on the lower portions of a bath tub or shower enclosure. Unlike the materials discussed to this point, cement board is not a gypsum product; it has a cement core covered with fiberglass mesh. One side is rough, the other is smooth (see the photo above). The rough side, designed for mortar application of tile, increases bonding and decreases tile slippage. The smooth side is for mastic application of tile.

Cement board is commonly available in $1/2$-in. and $5/8$-in. thick panels. Standard widths are 32 in., 36 in. and 48 in.; the standard length is 5 ft., although 8-ft. panels are also available. The maximum stud spacing for cement board is 16 in. o.c. Panels should be attached with special screws (or galvanized roofing nails), not with drywall screws or nails. (For more on installing cement board, see pp. 108-109.) Cement board is quite fragile and should be stored flat to prevent warping and should be handled as carefully as drywall.

Gypsum-core tile backer

Gypsum-core tile backer consists of a silicone-treated core covered with a glass mat on either side for added strength. The face has an acrylic coating, which serves as a vapor barrier. These panels, available in $1/2$-in. and $5/8$-in. thicknesses, are strong and lightweight and are easy to cut, snap and fasten. Gypsum-core tile backer is recommended for residential and light commercial use as an underlayment for ceramic tile. It is used in many of the same areas as cement board. Although not as durable as cement board, gypsum-core tile backer is easier to work with and is available in larger sizes (4x8 and 5x8). Framing specifications are the same as for cement board.

PLANNING THE JOB

Planning a drywall job involves more than just selecting the right type of drywall. You'll also need to estimate materials, make sure the materials will be available when needed (especially the longer-length panels), plan for access of the drywall and make sure you have enough help on the job site to maneuver the cumbersome panels. But before you start figuring out a material list for the job, there are some basic layout principles that you should keep in mind.

General layout guidelines

1. Always think of ways to eliminate unnecessary joints when planning the layout of a room. Use the longest panels possible; remember that most types of drywall are available in lengths up to 14 ft. or 16 ft. You may be tempted to use all 8-ft. lengths since they are lighter and easier to handle (and often cheaper), but don't. Using all 8-ft. panels creates too many seams that are difficult to hide. Keep in mind that fewer seams means less taping.

2. Ceiling panels can be attached either perpendicular to the ceiling joists (my preference) or parallel to the joists. Make sure the type of drywall you intend to use is approved for the stud or joist spacing; drywall is stronger in the long direction (see the sidebar on p. 52), and the framing spacing may affect the direction in which the drywall is hung.

3. Always try to avoid butted seams. A butted seam is a joint created when two untapered panel ends are joined together on the same framing member. If you have to use butted seams, stagger them as far from the center of the wall as possible. For example, if a wall is 8 ft. high by 20 ft. long, it would not be a good idea to use four 10-ft. panels (see the drawing at right). You'd end up with more than two butted seams on the wall or with seams on the same stud in the

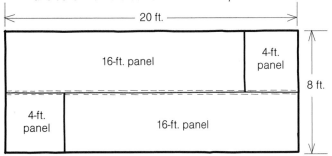

Butted seams (at the panel ends) are on different studs and as far from the center of the wall as possible.

The right way

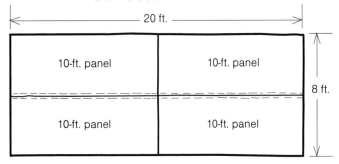

Butted seams are on the same stud and in the center of the wall.

Poorly placed butted seams

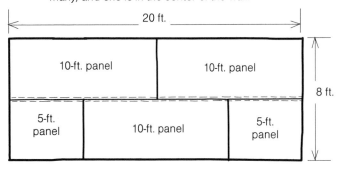

Butted seams are staggered, but there are too many, and one is in the center of the wall.

Too many butted seams

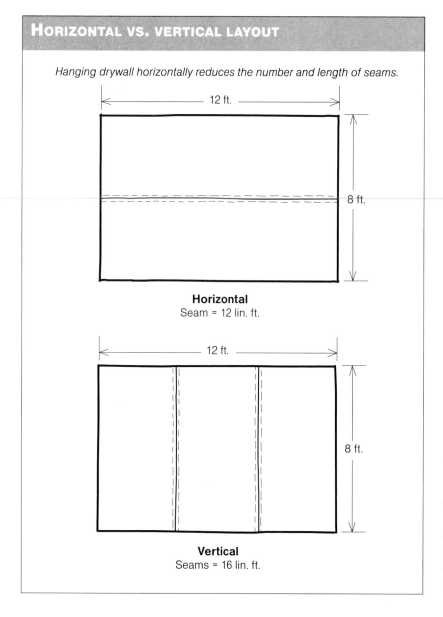

Hanging drywall horizontally reduces the number and length of seams.

12 ft.

8 ft.

Horizontal
Seam = 12 lin. ft.

12 ft.

8 ft.

Vertical
Seams = 16 lin. ft.

5. On walls that are over 4 ft. long and no more than 8 ft. high, hang the drywall horizontally (perpendicular to the studs). This technique reduces the linear footage of joints and also places the horizontal joints at a good height for taping (see the drawing at left).

6. On walls that are over 8 ft. high, consider using 54-in. wide drywall panels; they can greatly reduce the linear footage of seams.

Estimating materials

On most drywalling jobs, I figure a rough material list from the blueprints and job specifications. I use this information to estimate the cost of the job. Once the building is framed, I obtain my exact material list by measuring the actual walls and ceilings of the building.

Measuring the walls and ceilings makes it easier for me to visualize how I'll hang the drywall, what lengths and types I'll use—and where I'll use them. As I measure each room, I write down exactly what I'll need on a material list, using a separate list for each story of the building (see the sample material list on the facing page). The material list makes it easy to calculate the square footage of drywall that I'll need, which helps me figure a price for the entire job (I usually estimate a job by the square foot). From the square footage, I can figure the approximate amount of screws, nails, joint tape, joint compound and paint needed to complete the job (see the sidebar on p. 38).

When working up the material list, I usually round lengths of walls and ceilings to the next highest 2-ft. length panel. For example, if a wall is 12 ft. 9 in. long, I'd order a 14-ft. panel (see the top drawing on p. 14). The lower 4 ft. of the wall in this example is broken up by a doorway, so I'd order a 10-ft. panel to complete each side of the doorway with minimum waste. Always keep in

center of the wall. Instead, I would order two 16-footers and one 8-footer, arranged as shown in the drawing on p. 11. There are only two butted seams on the wall, and they're away from the center where they'll be easier to hide when taping and finishing.

4. On walls that are 4 ft. wide or less, hang the drywall parallel to the studs (standing on end) to avoid a seam.

Material List
Date:
Job Name:

Location:
Downstairs ☐   Upstairs ☐
Garage ☐   Other ☐

Regular Drywall ½"

Length	Total
8'	
10'	
12'	
14'	
16'	

Moisture Resistant ½"

Length	Total
8'	
10'	
12'	
14'	

Fire Resistant ⅝" ☐ ½" ☐

Length	Total
8'	
10'	
12'	
14'	

Other _____ Thickness _____

Length	Total
8'	
10'	
12'	
14'	

Corner Bead

Length	Total
8'	
10'	

Special instructions:

When filling out a material list, there are many ways to keep a tally of the number of sheets of drywall needed. I like to use the "dot tally" method; it takes up little space and doesn't require erasing if you make mistakes. Here's the key to the dot-tally system:

Symbol	Value	Symbol	Value
•	= 1	L̤	= 6
• •	= 2	U	= 7
⦙	= 3	☐	= 8
∷	= 4	⧄	= 9
⌐∷	= 5	⊠	= 10

If you put a dot in the wrong place, simply circle it. For example:

indicates 9, instead of 10.

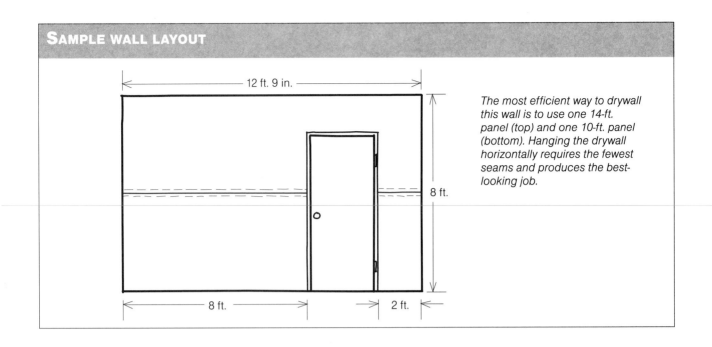

12 ft. 9 in.

8 ft.

8 ft.

2 ft.

The most efficient way to drywall this wall is to use one 14-ft. panel (top) and one 10-ft. panel (bottom). Hanging the drywall horizontally requires the fewest seams and produces the best-looking job.

SAMPLE ROOM ESTIMATE

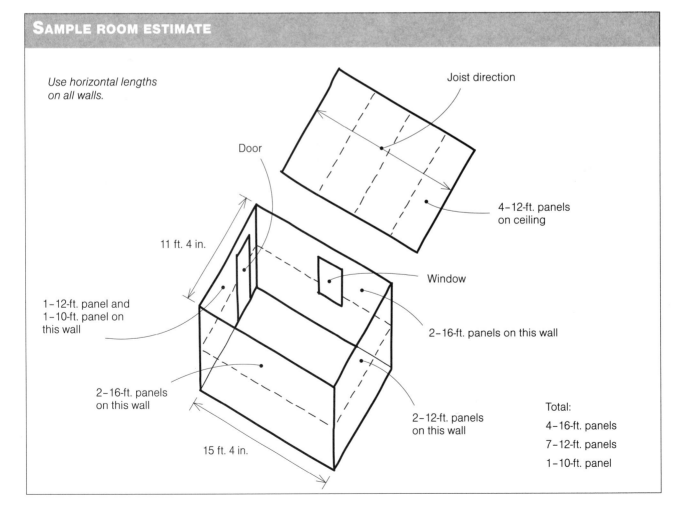

Use horizontal lengths on all walls.

Joist direction

Door

4–12-ft. panels on ceiling

11 ft. 4 in.

Window

1–12-ft. panel and 1–10-ft. panel on this wall

2–16-ft. panels on this wall

2–16-ft. panels on this wall

2–12-ft. panels on this wall

15 ft. 4 in.

Total:

4–16-ft. panels

7–12-ft. panels

1–10-ft. panel

mind that the idea is to use panels that span the entire length of the wall whenever possible.

The bottom drawing on the facing page shows how I'd estimate drywall for a whole room. In this particular example, I can use one length (16 ft.) for the wall with the window, since the window doesn't go all the way to the ceiling or floor and the wall is less than 16 ft. long. On the ceiling, I could use either three 16-ft. panels or four 12-ft. panels. In this example, I'd choose the four 12-footers because it's preferable to attach the panels perpendicular to the ceiling joists (see p. 52) and the shorter lengths are easier to handle.

Estimating materials for a whole house
When I'm working up a material list for a job, I usually don't need to figure a separate list for each room—I know that when I'm hanging the drywall, I'll use the maximum length possible for each wall. If I walk into a room that's 12x16, I know I'll be using mainly 12-ft. or 16-ft. long panels, unless a doorway allows me to use a shorter length.

As I walk through the house, I make a note of any rooms that will require special treatment. In the example shown in the plans on pp. 16-17, the upstairs master bedroom has a cathedral ceiling, so I'd have to make sure to allow extra drywall for the ceiling and the gable ends. Since it's not a good idea to plan a butted seam directly under the ridge beam on the ends of a cathedral ceiling (there could be structural weight and some movement or settling, which would eventually cause the seam to crack), I'd figure on spanning the end wall with 16-footers.

Cement board or tile backer will have to be used in the shower area of the master bathroom. I estimated the rest of the bathroom walls with ½-in. moisture resistant and ⅝-in. moisture resistant for the ceiling.

The garage ceiling joists are 24 in. o.c., so I estimated the whole ceiling with ⅝-in. fire-resistant drywall. All the garage walls adjacent to the house will need ⅝-in. fire resistant; in the rest of the garage I'd use regular ½-in. drywall. The garage walls are 10 ft. high, so I'd stand 10-footers on end to avoid any butted seams.

After tallying the number and types of drywall panels needed, the next step is to calculate the total square footage of drywall required. Multiply the number of panels needed for each length by the square footage in one panel, and then add all the totals together. For example, the total square footage of drywall needed for the house shown in the plans is calculated as shown in the chart below.

CALCULATING TOTAL SQUARE FOOTAGE

Length	# Panels Needed		Square Footage of Each Panel		Total Square Footage
8 ft.	40	x	32	=	1,280
10ft.	90	x	40	=	3,600
12 ft.	39	x	48	=	1,872
14 ft.	31	x	56	=	1,736
16 ft.	10	x	64	=	640
					9,128 sq. ft.

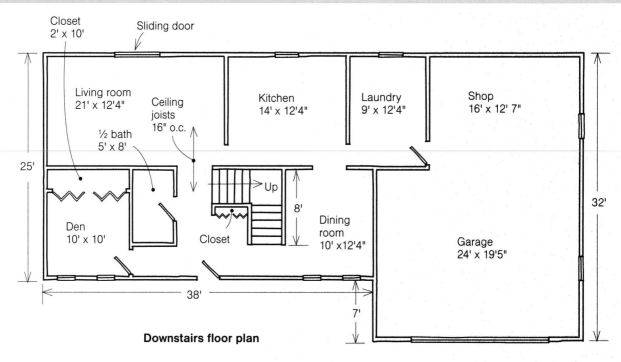

Closet
2' x 10'

Sliding door

Living room
21' x 12'4"

Ceiling
joists
16" o.c.

½ bath
5' x 8'

Kitchen
14' x 12'4"

Laundry
9' x 12'4"

Shop
16' x 12' 7"

25'

Den
10' x 10'

Up

Closet

8'

Dining
room
10' x12'4"

Garage
24' x 19'5"

32'

38'

7'

Downstairs floor plan

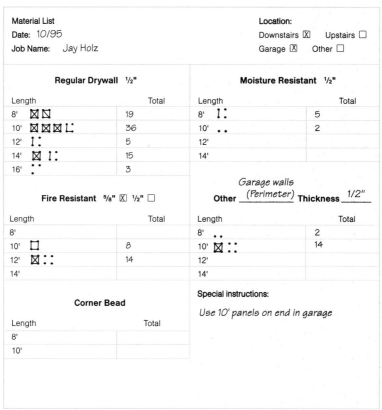

Material List
Date: 10/95
Job Name: Jay Holz

Location:
Downstairs ☒   Upstairs ☐
Garage ☒   Other ☐

Regular Drywall ½"		
Length		Total
8'	☒ ◩	19
10'	☒ ☒ ☒ ⌞	36
12'	Ⅰ ∴	5
14'	☒ Ⅰ ∴	15
16'	∴	3

Moisture Resistant ½"		
Length		Total
8'	Ⅰ ∴	5
10'	∙∙	2
12'		
14'		

Fire Resistant ⅝" ☒ ½" ☐		
Length		Total
8'		
10'	☐	8
12'	☒ ∷	14
14'		

Other Garage walls (Perimeter) Thickness 1/2"

Length		Total
8'	∙∙	2
10'	☒ ∷	14
12'		
14'		

Corner Bead		
Length		Total
8'		
10'		

Special instructions:

Use 10' panels on end in garage

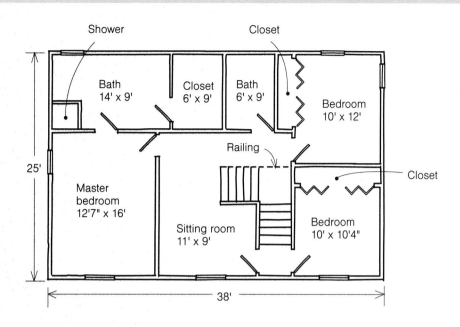

Upstairs floor plan

Material List	Location:
Date: 10/95	Downstairs ☐ Upstairs ☒
Job Name: Jay Holz	Garage ☐ Other ☐

Regular Drywall ½"		
Length		Total
8'	☒ ⠆	13
10'	☒ ☐	18
12'	☒ ⊔	17
14'	☒ ⠆	13
16'	⊔	7

Moisture Resistant ½"		
Length		Total
8'	⠁	1
10'	⊔	7
12'	⠆	3
14'	⠆	3

Fire Resistant ⅝" ☐ ½" ☐	
Length	Total
8'	
10'	
12'	
14'	

Other _Moisture Resistant_ **Thickness** _5/8"_		
Length		Total
8'		
10'	⠇	5
12'		
14'		

Corner Bead	
Length	Total
8'	
10'	

Special instructions:

Master Bedroom - cathedral ceiling - use 16' lengths

Bring baker's scaffold

Bathroom ceiling - 5/8" M.R.

Bathroom shower - get (3) 36"x 5' cement boards - 1/2" thick

Rough-estimating a house A quicker, though less accurate, way to estimate the amount of drywall needed for a house is to multiply the square footage of the living-area floor space for each story by 3.5. (I'd use this method to give a rough estimate over the phone, for example.) In the house in our example, multiplying the square footage of the upstairs and downstairs living areas (1,984 sq. ft.) by 3.5 would give a rough drywall total of 6,944 sq. ft. To this figure, we need to add the total for the garage. Multiply the total length of the garage walls by the height (112 ft. x 10 ft. = 1,120 sq. ft.), and then add the ceiling (approximately 700 sq. ft.): 1,120 + 700 = 1,820 sq. ft.

Using the rough estimating method, the total square footage of drywall needed for this house works out to be 8,764 sq. ft. (6,944 + 1,820). This figure is reasonably close to the actual square footage needed (9,128 sq. ft.)—and a lot quicker to calculate.

Planning for access of materials

When figuring a material list for any building, you need to consider what lengths you can get into the building and what's the best way to get the materials in (ideally, the contractor should start thinking about this before framing begins). For a normal single-story building, access is generally not a concern, but for anything over one story you may have to make some special arrangements.

To plan for the best access, measure and look over the job site before rough framing is complete. If necessary, ask the builder to leave out a window or a door, or even a section of plywood on an exterior wall to allow access for long panels. Look for any overhead wires that could get in the way of a boom-truck delivery. Also look for freshly covered ditches, or septic tanks, that might not support a heavy truck.

If special arrangements are being made, access may be available for only a limited time, so it's important to order unusual lengths or types of drywall ahead of time to prevent holdups that could delay the entire job. Also check out the job site to make sure there are appropriate areas to place all the drywall panels. The panels can be laid flat on the floor, or on edge against a wall (make sure they're almost straight so that they don't develop a bow). I like to distribute the panels in neat piles throughout the building to spread out the weight and speed up the hanging process.

Some time ago, my crew and I were drywalling the upstairs ceilings and walls in an old farmhouse. The only room finished upstairs was the master bedroom. Because the stairs were crooked and steep, the only length I'd be able to maneuver up them would be 8-footers. But I didn't want to use only 8-ft. panels, because the walls and ceilings were crooked and patched up, and there was quite a bit of loose plaster; if I'd used all 8-footers, I'd have ended up with a lot of difficult seams. The only way to get longer panels in (I wanted to use some 16-footers) was through a large window in the finished master bedroom.

Going through a finished room can be a customer's worst nightmare, so to avoid any damage to the master bedroom I had to cover the room with drop cloths and plastic and remove the window sashes. It took five of us approximately two hours to unload the truck and hand the panels through the window, but it was well worth it in the long run. It sounds like a lot of trouble to go to, but I ended up with a minimum number of seams, and the customer got the best possible job as a result.

Having enough help

Drywall panels are heavy, yet fragile and can be difficult to lift and move around without breaking. For that reason alone, many people use the shorter and lighter lengths. But if you have enough help, the longer panels are really not that difficult to carry and hang. (For tips on carrying drywall, see the sidebar on p. 47.)

Hanging 16-ft. panels on a ceiling usually takes three people; hanging 12-ft. panels on a wall takes two people. The best way to make use of the third person is to have him or her help with the longer panels as needed; the rest of the time, the helper can cut out electrical boxes, screw on the panels and hang the smaller pieces of drywall in the closets. (For more information on making the best use of helpers while hanging drywall, see pp. 47-48.)

If there's a large enough opening in an exterior wall, a drywall boom truck can make quick work of a second-story delivery.

If you don't have the luxury of second-story window access, the drywall's journey upstairs can be a little more circuitous.

TOOLS AND MATERIALS

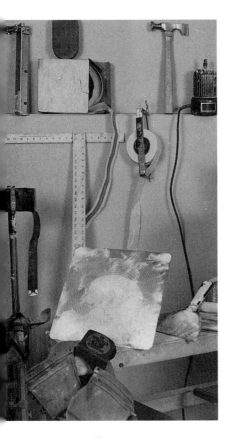

When I started out in the drywall business, I could easily carry in my arms all the tools that I would need to hang, tape and sand a drywalling job. My basic set of tools consisted of a T-square, a utility knife, a screwgun, a prybar, a utility saw, a wooden bench, four trowels and a hand sander. With these few basic tools, I was limited to relatively simple jobs—drywalling single rooms and small additions, repairing cracks and doing some minor remodeling—and I had to work pretty hard to get results that I was happy with.

As I gained experience and improved my techniques, I began to take on more challenging jobs—drywalling whole houses, working on high ceilings and hanging drywall on curved walls. These more difficult jobs required me to add tools (and manpower) to my drywalling arsenal, including a greater assortment of taping knives, adjustable work benches, and scaffolding. As well as adding tools, I've always tried to keep up with the latest developments in drywalling materials. Over the years, the types of fasteners, joint tapes and joint compounds have changed or been developed for specific uses.

You can do a pretty good job of drywalling with just the basic tools, but you'll get much better results—whether you're a professional or a homeowner—

if you have the right tools and materials. I've organized this chapter roughly in the order that each tool or material might be needed, starting with tools for measuring and marking on through tools for sanding. Rather than listing all the tools first and then listing the materials, I've combined the two categories—so, for example, you'll find screws and nails with the discussion of screwguns and hammers. I've also included some specialized tools (such as a drywall router, self-feeding screwgun attachment and corner crimper) that can make the job easier or faster. Keep in mind that many of these tools can be rented at a tool rental store.

HANGING TOOLS

There are probably more tools required for hanging drywall than for any other step in the process. To do a good job, you'll need an assortment of measuring and marking tools, various cutting tools, tools for lifting and supporting drywall panels, and tools and materials for fastening drywall. Depending on the height of the ceilings, you might also need to use scaffolding.

Measuring and marking tools

Taking accurate measurements is a very important part of drywalling. If you measure a panel too short, you'll have to do some extra patching at the taping stage

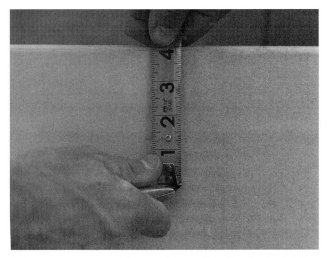

A tape measure can be used to scribe short, straight measurements. Pinch the tape at the desired dimension along the edge of the panel, and scribe a line with a utility knife as you ride the tape along the panel.

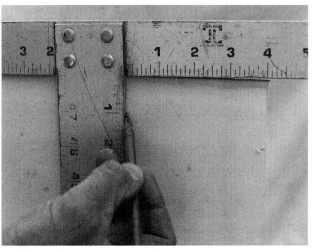

When marking narrow strips of drywall or squaring up the end of a panel, line up the desired measurement along the top edge of the square.

(see the sidebar on p. 71). If you measure a panel too long and force it into place, the ends will break apart, again requiring additional patching. For accurate measurements, I rely on a 25-ft. tape measure. You'll need a tape that long for figuring materials for large rooms. A 25-ft. tape is a little wider and stiffer than shorter-length tapes and extends farther before it bends or sags, which makes it easier to measure long lengths by yourself. Regardless of length, tape measures are also useful for scribing short, straight measurements, as shown in the photo above.

A 4-ft. aluminum T-square, which is used both for marking and cutting drywall, is one tool that you really can't do without. In use, the top edge of the square is butted against the long tapered edge of the drywall panel and the 4-ft. piece hangs down along the face of the panel at 90° (the square can also be used as a straightedge for angled cuts). The edges of the square are calibrated in inches. When marking straight, narrow pieces of drywall, locate the measurement you

want on the top edge of the T-square and line it up with the panel edge (see the photo above). Then mark the panel with a pencil or score it with a utility knife. ("Scoring" means cutting through the paper surface of the panel.)

A 24-in. framing square also comes in handy for marking and cutting drywall. I use this square mostly for transferring measurements when cutting out small openings (for electrical boxes, heat-duct openings, and so forth) after a panel is attached (see the photos on p. 45).

A chalkline is used for marking straight lines, primarily for lines that are difficult to scribe with a tape measure and knife or too long to mark with a 4-ft. square. To mark a line between two points, hook the end of the chalkline over the mark on one end of the panel and stretch the line to the other mark. Pull the line tight, and with your other hand lift the string straight up from the surface a few inches and release. The colored chalk from the string will leave a mark on the surface. When marking a

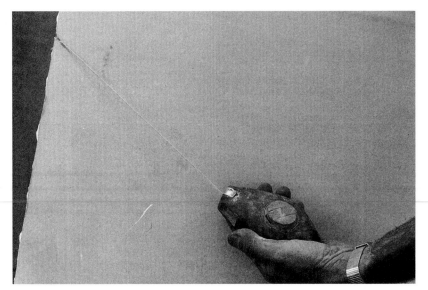

straight line for angled cuts, the hook on the end of the line has an annoying habit of slipping off the edge of the panel. If you don't have anyone to hold the end in place, make a cut about ¼ in. deep at the mark and slide the hooked end of the string into the cut (see the photo at left).

A scriber, which is similar to a drafting compass, is used to fit out-of-plumb walls (see the sidebar below), to mark round openings (see p. 46) and to fit irregular surfaces. When fitting an irregular surface, such as a very wavy ceiling, hold the drywall panel as tightly as possible against the irregular surface, place the metal point of the scriber against the surface at a right angle, and then follow along the contour. As you slide the

When marking an angled line with a chalkline, hook the end of the string into a small notch in the drywall to prevent it from slipping.

FITTING A SQUARE PANEL INTO AN OUT-OF-PLUMB CORNER

A square-cut panel will not fit properly against a wall that's not plumb. To compensate for the out-of-plumb corner, cut the panel about an inch or so long and then position it in the corner. Run the point of a scriber (held roughly at a right angle) along the out-of-plumb wall to mark the cutting line, and cut to fit.

Butt the panel against the corner.

Run the scriber along the out-of-plumb wall to mark the edge of the panel.

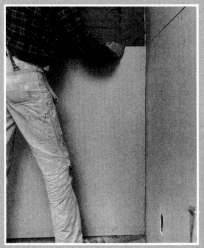

The cut panel should fit snugly into the corner.

scriber along the ceiling, the pencil end will leave a mark on the panel that will be cut to fit. Cut along the pencil line with a utility knife or saw.

Cutting tools

It's not often that you'll hang a piece of drywall without having to make some sort of cut. You may need to cut the panel to length or width, or make an opening for an electrical outlet box, a window or a door. On some panels you may have to make more than one cut. The tools described in this section will help you make clean, accurate cuts in any type of drywall.

The most commonly used cutting tool is a utility knife. It is typically used in combination with a 4-ft. square to make cuts across the full width of a panel, though it can be used to cut along the mark left by a chalkline. To cut a panel using a utility knife, first mark the length of the panel and then cut through the face paper and into the gypsum core (see the photo at right below). Next, snap the panel back away from the cut line and make a second cut along the crease from the back side. Snap the panel forward again and the two pieces will separate cleanly.

The sharper the knife blade and the deeper the cut, the smoother the cut edge will be—if the knife is sharp, one stroke on either side of the panel will be all that you need. A dull blade will leave a jagged cut that may leave the panel a little longer than measured (see the

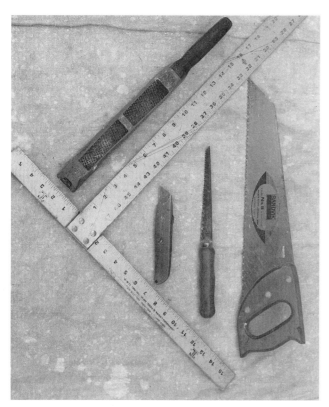

Tools for cutting drywall include (from right to left) a drywall saw, a utility saw, a utility knife (usually used with a 4-ft. T-square) and a rasp.

To make a cut across the full width of a panel, score the paper with a utility knife along the edge of a T-square.

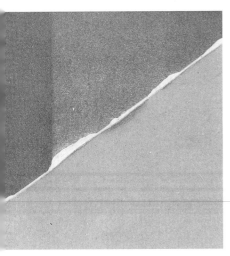

A dull blade in a utility knife can leave a jagged cut edge.

photo at left). The jagged edge can be trimmed off with a utility knife, or, for a better job, it can be smoothed out with a drywall rasp.

Saws Customers are sometimes surprised to see me using a saw to cut drywall, but in certain instances it's faster and easier to use than a utility knife. The teeth in drywall saws have more "set" in them than standard wood-cutting handsaws (the set is determined by the amount the teeth are bent out in each direction—the wider the set, the wider the kerf taken out with the saw). The wide-set teeth rip through the paper and gypsum core quite easily, and the wide kerf also helps prevent damage to the paper surface when the sawblade is drawn back.

There are two different types of saws for cutting drywall. I use the smaller drywall utility saw to cut openings for electrical outlets, pipes and ducts and to cut square pieces out of panels. The saw has a sharp pointed end, making it easy to start a cut in the center of a panel. I use the larger drywall saw, which is stiffer than an ordinary wood saw, to cut along a door or window opening after the drywall has been hung over the opening and tacked in place. (Make this cut only if the door or window jambs have not been installed—otherwise, you'll damage the jambs; see p. 44.) The drywall saw also works well for trimming panels that are run a little long at outside corners or at the edge of a doorway. Another use for this rigid saw is to make beveled cuts, which are sometimes necessary for a good fit at corners that are greater than 90°.

Drywall router A drywall router is a specialized tool that's great for cutting out small openings in drywall panels. A specially designed router bit cuts through the drywall as it follows along the edge of an electrical box or a heat-duct opening. Cutting openings with a router requires less-accurate measurements than cutting with a saw, because you need to find only one edge and follow it around (see pp. 45-47). If you use this tool, be sure to apply only light pressure—with too much pressure the bit could cut right through a plastic electrical box.

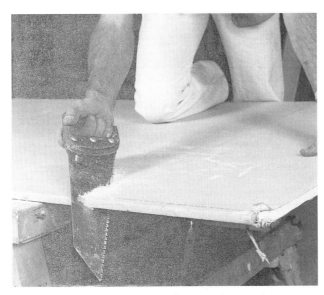

A drywall saw is the best tool to use for cutting a beveled edge.

A drywall router is a specialized tool for cutting out electrical boxes and other small openings.

Lifting tools

All drywall panels have to be lifted into place before they are attached. Sometimes they may only have to be held about ½ in. off the floor; at other times they may need to be hoisted to the top of a cathedral ceiling.

When hanging drywall on a wall horizontally (my preferred method of working), the top panel can be lifted into place by hand and nailed or screwed home. The bottom panel is then set into place and lifted up to butt against the bottom of the top sheet, usually less than 1 in. off the floor. You can use a small prybar to hold the panel off the floor, but this tool usually requires the use of one or both hands. I prefer to use a panel lifter, which can be operated with your foot, leaving both hands free to attach the panel.

On flat ceilings, a T-support is a handy tool for holding a panel in place, freeing up your hands for fastening. This simple prop can be made out of furring strip or a 2x4 with a 4-ft. long furring strip screwed to the top. It's best to make the T-support on the job to fit the height of the ceiling (I make mine about a ½ in. longer than the ceiling height so it will fit snugly).

Hanging drywall is usually a job for two or more people, but a drywall lift (available from tool rental stores) makes it possible for one person to hang drywall alone. The lift adjusts for different-height walls and ceilings (sloped as well as flat) and for different-length panels. The panel is placed finished face toward the lift. For ceiling attachment, begin by positioning the panel roughly, with one end tilted up slightly. Position the panel exactly as you crank up the lift, and leave the lift in place until the edges are fastened.

A simple T-support can really help when you need a free pair of hands for fastening.

A panel lifter is a handy tool for raising a drywall panel an inch or so off the floor. The panel goes on the end with the tab and is raised into place when you step on the other end.

A drywall lift is a specialized tool for hanging drywall.

Drywall benches provide a stable step and platform when attaching ceilings.

Step-up benches or trestles are typically used for ceilings up to about 9 ft. high. These stable aluminum benches are about 4 ft. long and 10 in. wide and are adjustable in height from about 18 in. to 32 in. The horizontal supports can be used as a step when climbing up onto the bench with a drywall panel (see the photo at left) or to support a short plank stretched between two benches. The bench should be adjusted to a height that places your head close to the ceiling; after the panel is lifted into place, it can be held there with light head pressure, and both hands are free to attach the panel.

For ceilings that are too high for benches, a baker's scaffold provides a nice, stable, adjustable platform (see the photo at left below). Scaffolds are available in 6-ft.,

8-ft. and 10-ft. lengths and are adjustable up to 6 ft. high. Some baker's scaffolds can be stacked two sections high. A single section can be guided through most doorways, so it doesn't need to be disassembled if you want to move it from room to room.

For higher ceilings or walls, a stable platform is a must. The scaffold should be at least 4 ft. wide and 10 ft. long, and it should be adjustable at least every 15 in. or so—with horizontal end supports so that you can run planks at different heights (see the photo below). Working on any type of scaffolding demands attention to safety; the sidebar on the facing page lists some important safety considerations.

An adjustable baker's scaffold provides stable support when installing drywall ceilings up to heights of about 12 ft.

A drywall scaffold should be strong and stable and have crossbars at the ends at least every 15 in.

• The floor supporting any scaffolding should be sound, rigid and capable of carrying the load without settling or displacement. Any scaffold damaged or weakened should be repaired immediately.

• Scaffolds 4 ft. to 10 ft. high should have standard guardrails on all open sides and ends of the platform. Guardrails should be made of lumber no smaller than 2x4 and installed 42 in. above the platform surface, with a midrail of 1x6 lumber.

• Any platform over 10 ft. high should have toeboards as well as guardrails on all open sides and ends. Toeboards should be at least 4 in. high and extend around the perimeter of the platform.

• Scaffold planks should extend over the end supports at least 6 in. and should be laid with the edges close together.

• If you are working in an area where there is any risk of head injury, you should wear an approved hard hat.

Stilts I use stilts primarily when I'm taping and sanding, but some pros like to use them when hanging drywall, too. Stilts eliminate the need for benches and scaffolding on ceilings 9 ft. high or lower, and allow a lot of mobility. They make it easy to apply long lengths of joint tape and to finish an entire seam at one go, thereby helping to increase job productivity and the quality of work. (Note that safety regulations in some states do not allow the use of stilts, and many insurance policies do not cover workers who are injured while on stilts.)

When I bought my first pair of stilts, it took me a few weeks to summon up the courage to use them. I was afraid I'd make a fool of myself in front of a customer (and in front of my workmates!). But when I finally tried the stilts, it didn't take too long to get the hang of them. It's so much easier (and faster) to work on stilts than to drag around benches and ladders, and as long as you keep all work areas clean, probably safer too. Now I use stilts not only for taping and

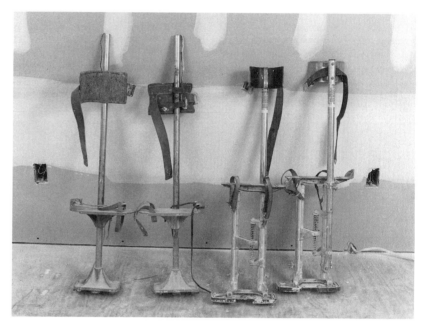

Most stilts are adjustable for different heights. The pair on the right also has joints that flex with ankle movement.

A drywall screwgun and hammer are the best tools for fastening drywall. To minimize the risk of tearing the face paper, it's better to use a convex-faced drywall hammer (at right) rather than a standard, flat-faced carpenter's hammer (at center).

A self-feeding screwgun attachment greatly speeds up the process of fastening drywall.

sanding, but also for insulating ceilings and for cutting in with a paint brush along ceiling edges.

Fastening tools and materials

Drywall can be hung with nails or screws. If you use nails, you'll need a drywall hammer, which looks a little like a hatchet. The blade end is tapered (but not sharp) so it can be used for prying or lifting. The face of the hammer is convex, which leaves a shallow dimple in the face of the drywall without tearing the face paper (a standard carpenter's hammer has a flat face, which can easily tear the paper). The dimple is concealed with joint compound during the taping process.

Nowadays, most professional drywallers use screws rather than nails, and the drywall screwgun has replaced the hammer as the tool of choice for attaching drywall. A screwgun installs a screw with a bugle head just below the surface of the drywall paper. It has a positive clutch that is engaged when pressure is applied to the Phillips bit. The depth of the screw bit is adjustable; when properly adjusted, the screwgun sets the screw just below the surface without tearing the face paper.

Screwing is faster than nailing, but having to place every screw onto the bit by hand can be time-consuming (and tedious). One way around this problem is to buy a special attachment that feeds the screws automatically. A string of screws feeds into the nosepiece as each screw is used, greatly increasing productivity. Self-feeding screwgun attachments are available to fit most brands of screwguns; they accept screws from 1 in. to 1¾ in. long.

Screws and nails Fastening drywall with screws is preferred over nailing because screws are faster to install than nails, they do less damage to the drywall panel and they hold the drywall tighter against

FASTENER SPECIFICATIONS		
Fastener Type	**Drywall Thickness**	**Minimum Fastener Length**
Wood screws (coarse thread)	⅜ in.	1 in.
	½ in.	1⅛ in.
	⅝ in.	1¼ in.
Screws into metal studs or furring (fine thread)	⅜ in.	¾ in.
	½ in.	⅞ in.
	⅝ in.	1 in.
Ring-shank nails (wood studs only)	⅜ in.	1⅛ in.
	½ in.	1¼ in.
	⅝ in.	1⅜ in.

the framing. Screws for wood framing should be long enough to penetrate the framing at least ⅝ in. (see the chart above). Screws for metal framing, which have finer threads than wood-framing screws, should penetrate at least ⅜ in. (Note that you should always use screws in metal studs—nails will not hold.)

If you use nails, they should penetrate the wood framing at least ¾ in. Ring-shank nails are preferred over plain-shank nails because they have 25% greater holding power. (The holding power is greatly diminished if the drywall face is damaged, so be careful not to tear the paper or sink the nail too deep, which can severely damage the gypsum core.)

Outside-corner protection Panels hung on outside corners not only require attachment with screws or nails, but also some form of protection or reinforcement at the corners. Metal corner beads are the most common form of protection for outside corners, uncased openings, beams and soffits. The exposed bead resists impact and forms a straight raised

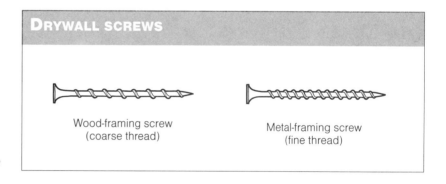

DRYWALL SCREWS

Wood-framing screw (coarse thread)

Metal-framing screw (fine thread)

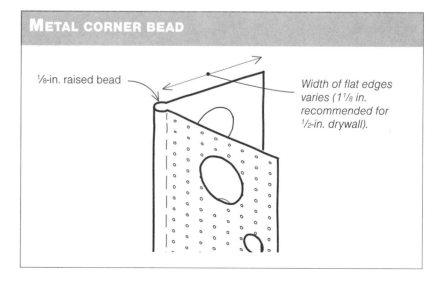

METAL CORNER BEAD

⅛-in. raised bead

Width of flat edges varies (1⅛ in. recommended for ½-in. drywall).

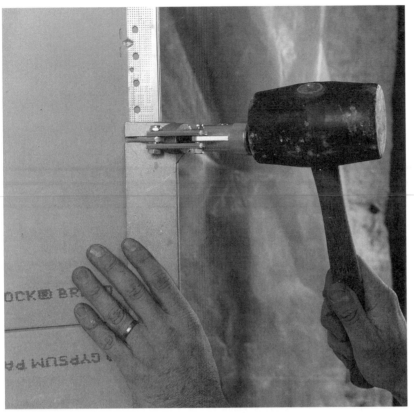

One blow with a rubber mallet on a corner crimper every 4 in. to 6 in. attaches metal corner bead securely to an outside corner.

edge that can be followed as a screed when taping (see p. 72). Metal corner beads should be installed in one piece unless the length of the corner exceeds standard corner-bead length (6 ft. 10 in., 8 ft. and 10 ft.).

You can use nails or screws to attach the corner bead, but it's much faster to work with a corner crimper (see the photo at left). With the corner bead in position, hold the crimper against the metal corner and strike it with a rubber mallet. The blow causes the metal blades to crimp the flat edges of the corner bead into the drywall.

Flexible corner beads, which are made of vinyl and available in 10-ft. lengths, are used to protect outside corners of archways and curved window openings. One edge of the corner bead is notched every inch (see the photo at left below). As the bead is placed along a curved area, the notches spread apart a little, while the solid inside edge flexes along the arch. (A metal corner bead can be

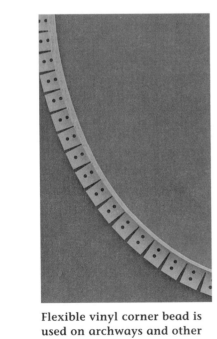

Flexible vinyl corner bead is used on archways and other curved openings.

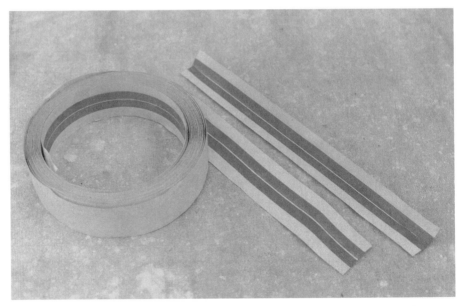

Flexible metal corner tape is used on outside corners that form an angle greater than 90° and in repair work for straightening inside corners.

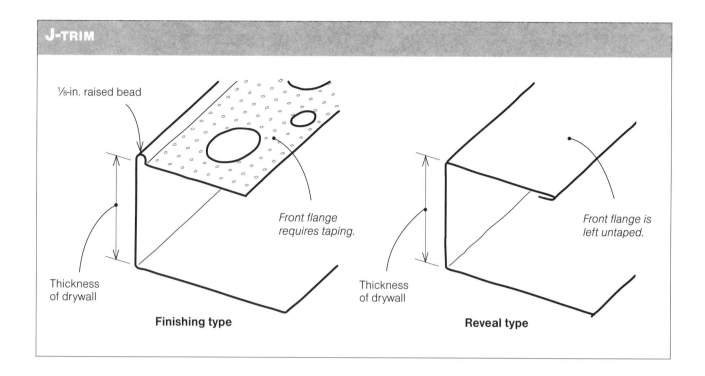

⅛-in. raised bead

Thickness of drywall

Finishing type

Front flange requires taping.

Thickness of drywall

Reveal type

Front flange is left untaped.

notched in a similar fashion, but it is harder to work with and the metal kinks easily.)

Flexible metal corner tape is used on outside corners that are greater than 90° and do not have adequate framing for attaching regular metal corner bead. (Flexible tape is used on inside corners only to straighten out a crooked or badly damaged corner in repair work.) Available in rolls 2 in. wide and 100 ft. long, this tape is like regular paper tape (see pp. 34-35) except that it is reinforced with a ½-in. wide galvanized metal strip running along both sides of the center crease (see the bottom right photo on the facing page). It forms a stronger and straighter corner than plain paper tape. The metal tape is embedded in joint compound with the metal side facing in and finished like any other corner. As with regular metal corner bead, it can be cut to length with tin snips.

Metal or plastic J-trims are caps that are used to cover the edge of a drywall panel. Typical applications are against a shower stall, a window jamb or a brick wall, or around an opening that is left untrimmed. The J-trim can be installed before hanging the panel or after the panel is loosely attached. It is held in place by driving a nail or screw through the face of the drywall and through the longer back flange of the J-trim. J-trim is available in different thicknesses to fit different thicknesses of drywall, and in types that need to be finished with joint compound and types that require no finishing (see the drawing above).

TAPING TOOLS AND MATERIALS

It used to be that you could buy a couple of trowels, a roll of paper tape and a pail of joint compound and you would have everything available to do a typical taping job. Nowadays, there are a lot of types and sizes of trowels, paper tape is not the only choice for reinforcing seams, and there are so many different types of joint compounds that you may not know where to begin when deciding which to use.

TROWEL CARE

• **In use, keep trowels free of dry joint compound to avoid marks or scratches when trying to smooth the compound. Use another trowel (or the edge of the hawk) to scrape off any excess compound. When you've finished a taping session, clean trowels with warm water.**

• **Use trowels for taping only. Don't scrape floors or apply adhesive or tile grout with your taping tools.**

• **Protect edges from nicks or scratches; any nicks should be sanded or filed out smooth.**

• **Round any sharp corners on a new trowel with a file (sharp corners can rip the joint tape).**

The four types of trowels used for taping are (counterclockwise from right) taping knives, a curved or beveled trowel, a hawk and a straight-handled trowel.

Trowels

There are four types of trowels for taping, all available in different sizes for different applications. As I discuss each trowel, I'll mention the size that I use most often and, where appropriate, explain what features to look for when purchasing a trowel. I'll explain how to use each trowel in greater detail in Chapter 4.

Taping knives Taping knives, available in widths from 1 in. to 6 in. (in 1-in. increments), are used for taping seams and corners and covering fasteners. The wider widths often have a metal end on the handle for resetting nail heads. Narrower widths come in handy for taping tight areas (for example, the sometimes narrow space between a door frame and a corner). I use a 6-in. knife more than any other size. Whatever the width of the trowel, it

should be fairly stiff; it should have some "give" but not be too flexible. Cheaper, flimsier trowels are hard to work with and tend to leave too much joint compound on the surface. Stiffer knives give you more control and are less prone to nicks and bending. I usually round off the corners off a new knife with a file; sharp corners can tear the paper tape or leave grooves in the joint compound.

When buying a taping knife, look for one that has a little curve in the blade when viewed from head on. If you can't find one, you can put a slight curve in the blade by bending it over a rounded surface such as a pipe. I use the convex side of the blade when taping, and the curve helps keep the corners of the blade slightly away from the taping surface, resulting in a smooth surface without the ridges created by a flat taping-knife blade.

A hawk is used for holding large amounts of joint compound when taping with a knife.

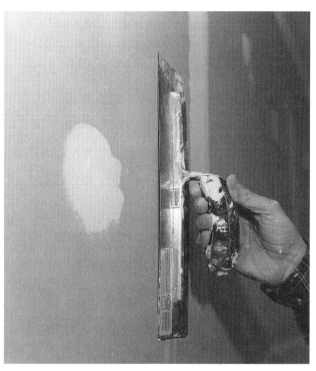

A beveled trowel has a slight curve in the blade, which allows better feathering and finishing of seams.

A square-cornered taping knife cannot reach into a corner very well if the corner is less than 90° (for example, where a sloped ceiling and a wall intersect or at the top of a cellar stairway). In these areas, I use a pointed trowel, which can easily be made by cutting off the sides of an old 6-in. taping knife. A small pointed mason's trowel would also work fine for this purpose.

Hawks A hawk is used to hold large quantities of joint compound when working with a taping knife. The tool has a square aluminum top, with circular grooves to help prevent the joint compound from sliding off, and a short, straight handle centered on the underside. Hawks are available in sizes from 8 in. to 14 in. square. I prefer to work with the largest size.

Curved or beveled trowels Curved or beveled trowels have a slight curve in the blade about $\frac{5}{32}$ in. deep. They are available in lengths from 10 in. to 14 in., and in 4-in. and $4\frac{1}{2}$-in. widths. I prefer to use a beveled trowel rather than a flat trowel because the curve helps me to finish seams to an inconspicuous crown.

I use the $4\frac{1}{2}$-in. by 14-in. beveled trowel for feathering and finishing most seams. I also use this larger trowel for holding joint compound while applying the compound with a taping knife. It has many uses, and I always seem to have a beveled trowel and a 6-in. taping knife in my hand while taping.

A 12-in. straight-handled trowel is used primarily for smoothing out the final coat of joint compound.

Precreased paper tape is the best tape to use for inside corners and butted seams.

Fiberglass-mesh tape is the tape of choice for reinforcing tapered seams and patching small holes.

Wide straight-handled taping trowels
Wide straight-handled taping trowels are much the same as taping knifes, except that they have a wooden handle that extends over the blade for greater rigidity (some have a metal reinforcing strip at the back of the blade). They are used for smoothing out the final thin coat of joint compound on seams or outside corners, and for smoothing out large areas or intersections of seams. Straight-handled taping trowels are available in widths from 10 in. to 24 in. As with taping knives, they should have a slight curve in the blade and the corners should be rounded with a file. I use a 12-in. trowel for most applications.

Joint tape
Joint tape is used to reinforce seams and corners, and also to repair cracks or holes in drywall or plaster. There are two types of tape: precreased paper tape and fiberglass-mesh tape.

Paper tape Not long ago, paper tape was the only tape you could buy. It is still widely used and is a good all-round tape for seams, cracks and small holes. Available in rolls 2 in. wide and 250 ft. to 500 ft. long, paper tape has a light crease down the center, which helps it fold easily for use on inside corners. Although mesh tape has largely supplanted paper tape for finishing tapered edge seams, paper tape still has a number of advantages and uses. First, paper tape is stronger than mesh and not as likely to be torn by taping tools. It also resists stretching and wrinkling more effectively. And paper tape works much better than mesh for inside corners—the crease makes it easier to keep the tape centered and straight. Finally, paper tape is cheaper than mesh. On the downside, paper tape is more time-consuming to apply (it has to be embedded in a coat of compound) and prone to bubbling if not enough compound is used.

Fiberglass-mesh tape Fiberglass-mesh tape is commonly used for taping tapered seams and patching cracks and small holes. It is also used to reinforce gaps between panels or in corners that are over ¼ in. wide. Mesh tape is not recommended for inside corners, because it is hard to keep centered and straight and is easy to cut through with a trowel when finishing corners (or to sand through in areas where only a thin layer of compound has been applied).

Fiberglass-mesh tape comes in rolls 1½ in. or 2 in. wide by 300 ft. long. There are two types: self-adhesive tape, which is simply pressed in place over a seam, and non-adhesive (or plain) tape. The non-adhesive type is less expensive but is not as easy to work with as the self-adhesive (it has to be stapled in place over a seam). Either type can be cut with a utility knife or with the sharp edge of a trowel. One important point when using self-adhesive tape: Always store opened rolls in a plastic bag between uses to prevent the tape from drying out and losing its adhesiveness.

If you're taping a lot of seams, a handy tool to have at your side is a tape reel (also known as a tape holder). The reel, which attaches to your belt, can hold up to a 500-ft. roll and works with both paper and mesh tape. The tape rolls off the reel for quick and easy tear-offs.

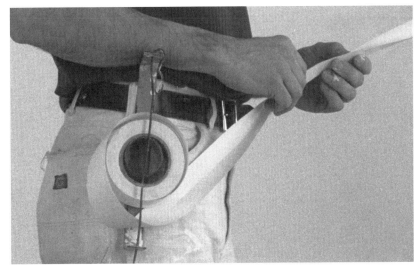

A tape reel is a handy dispenser for paper or mesh tape.

Joint compound

There are so many different types and brands of joint compound on the market that it can be difficult to know what to use. The most important distinction is between drying-type compounds and setting-type compounds. In this section, I'll describe some of the most popular types within the two categories.

Drying-type joint compound Drying-type compound is the more common of the two—it's the type you'll see in buckets at your local hardware store. It is available premixed and in powdered form. Premixed drying-type joint compounds come in 1-gal. and 5-gal. buckets. The 1-gal. size is good for patching small jobs; the 5-gal. bucket will tape the average 12-ft. by 12-ft. room.

The main advantage of using premixed compounds is that they are ready to use right out of the bucket. The consistency of the mix is factory controlled, and most brands are equal in quality. Also, there is little waste with premixed compounds—the bucket can be resealed and used again later. When working with premixed compound, the fresher the compound the better. Buckets should be kept out of direct sunlight, and the compound should never be allowed to freeze. Premixed compound will not keep indefinitely, especially after it's been opened; at room temperature, an opened pail of compound will start to go bad in about a month.

Powdered drying-type joint compounds have all the same working characteristics as premixed compounds. The major difference is that they come in dry form and require mixing with water. The dry compound can be stored at any temperature for extended periods (though it should always be warmed to room temperature before mixing).

I use three kinds of drying-type joint compound on a regular basis: taping compound, topping compound and all-purpose joint compound (each is available premixed or dry). *Taping* compound is used to embed the joint tape for the first coat and as a filler in the second coat (explained in Chapter 4). It is a strong compound with little shrinkage as it dries, and excellent bond and resistance to cracking. *Topping* compound is used for the thin finishing coat. It is easy to work with, feathers out nicely, dries quickly and sands smooth.

Topping compound can be used over taping compound or over all-purpose joint compound.

As its name suggests, *all-purpose* compound can be used for all stages of the taping process—to embed the tape, as a filler coat and as a finish coat. Because it's more convenient to deal with just one type, all-purpose compound is the most commonly used compound. However, it doesn't have the same strength, binding qualities or stability as the taping and topping combination.

All drying-type compounds require an application temperature of at least 55°F (surface, compound and air temperature). The compound must dry thoroughly between coats, and the drying time will be greatly affected by temperature, humidity and airflow. Under good conditions, drying-type compounds will dry within 24 hours.

Setting-type joint compound While drying-type compounds are vinyl-based and dry as the water evaporates, setting-type compounds harden by chemical reaction. The great advantage of setting-type compounds, which are available in powdered form only, is that they harden faster than drying-type compounds.

CHOOSING THE RIGHT JOINT COMPOUND

When deciding which type of joint compound to use, consider the following factors:

• The size of the job (for a small job, it is less convenient to use two or three types of compound).

• The drying and heating conditions (temperature, airflow and humidity).

• The availability of materials, including the availability of water on the job. Taping compound and some of the faster-drying setting-type compounds are available only at larger drywall-supply stores.

• The amount of time you have to complete the job (use setting types if time is short).

• The recommended combination of products (for example, mesh tape should be embedded in a taping compound or setting-type compound).

• Personal preferences (whether you prefer the convenience of the premixed drying type, or the strength and better bonding of the setting type).

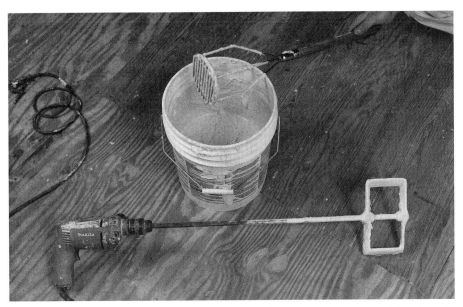

Joint compound can be mixed with a powered mixing paddle or with a hand mixer.

Setting times vary from 20 minutes to 6 hours, depending on the type used. The type I prefer to use sets up in about 3 to 4 hours, which allows me enough time to apply the compound to the seams and know that it will be ready for the next coat of compound by the next day, even in humid or cool conditions (air, surface and compound temperature can be as low as 45°F with setting types). Further, setting-type compound can be second- and third-coated as soon as it sets up—you don't have to wait until it is completely dry. Other benefits of setting-type compounds are that they have better bonding qualities, they don't shrink and crack much when drying, and they produce a harder finish.

Given that setting-type compounds have so many advantages, you might wonder why anyone would use anything else. But there is a downside: The stuff is much harder to sand than drying-type compound, which means that you have to get it as smooth as possible while tap-ing (there is, however, a lightweight setting-type compound that is easier to

sand than the stronger, standard setting type). Also, you should mix only as much compound as you can use before it sets up—unlike powdered drying-type com-pounds, it cannot be stored and reused at a later date.

For most of my work, I like to use a setting-type compound to embed the tape (first coat). I'll often use the same type of compound for the second, filler coat, making sure to take the time to get the compound as smooth as possible. For the third and final coat, I use a drying-type compound—either an all-purpose or a topping compound.

Mixing tools Joint compound can be mixed with a powered paddle or by hand (see the photo above and the discussion on pp. 62-64). Mixing paddles are used with a heavy-duty 1/2-in. electric drill for thorough mixing of joint compounds (and textured finishes). A hand mixer is excellent for mixing ready-mixed com-pounds that have sat too long or been thinned down with water for ease of application.

APPROXIMATE COVERAGE OF MATERIALS

SCREWS AND NAILS
The number of fasteners used to attach drywall varies depending on framing spacing, fastener spacing, panel length and panel orientation. For rough estimating, I usually figure around 1,000 fasteners for 1,000 sq. ft. of drywall.

JOINT TAPE
It usually takes about 370 lin. ft. of joint tape to finish 1,000 sq. ft. of drywall.

JOINT COMPOUND
The amounts figured below are estimates for the complete taping job (three coats):

• Premixed drying-type joint compound—11 gal. for 1,000 sq. ft. of drywall.

• Powdered drying-type compound—80 lb. of dry compound mixed with water for 1,000 sq. ft. of drywall. (Powdered compound is usually sold in 25-lb. bags.)

• Setting-type joint compounds vary in weight by types. A rough guide is to figure about 3 bags of dry compound for 1,000 sq. ft. of drywall.

Tools for sanding drywall include a dry sanding sponge (left), a pole sander (center), a hand sander (right) and a sanding screen (front).

SANDING TOOLS AND MATERIALS

Sanding is the final stage in the dry-walling process. You can sand joint compound with a piece of folded sandpaper, but there are a number of tools that can make this unpleasant (but important) task go a little faster and improve the quality of the job.

Sanders
I use a pole sander for most sanding work. The sander has a pivoting head designed to hold precut sanding screens or drywall sandpaper. The 4-ft.-long handle helps you reach along the top edge of a wall or near the floor without having to stretch or bend too much. Most low ceilings can also be reached from the floor with a pole sander. Grasp the handle with both hands for better leverage.

For areas that are easier to reach or that are too tight for a pole sander, a hand sander is a good alternative. It's the same size as a pole sander (with a 4-in. by 8-in. head), but without the pole.

For the extra fine sanding work that is necessary after sanding with a pole or hand sander, I like to use a dry sanding sponge. The small, dense sponge, which measures about 3 in. by 4 in. by 1 in. thick, is coated with grit. Dry sanding sponges are available in fine, medium and coarse grit; I prefer the fine grit for touch-up sanding. Don't confuse this sanding sponge with the drywall sponge that is used wet (see p. 39).

To get into the tight spots that even a sanding sponge won't reach, I use a folded piece of sandpaper. Sandpaper works especially well on inside corners and allows the best control of any sanding method.

For jobs where clouds of dust are unacceptable, a wet drywall sponge is the answer. The sponge shown in the photo

A wet sanding sponge cuts down on the amount of dust produced during the sanding process.

above is a high-density polyurethane sponge that is soft and non-abrasive. Sponges are good for blending the edges of taped areas and small defects, but they are not as effective on ridges or for smoothing down built-up areas. If you intend to finish-sand with a wet sponge, you really have to do a good taping job. Note that for wet-sanding small areas, you could use an all-purpose household sponge or even a smooth, soft cloth.

Sanding materials

You can sand joint compound with regular sandpaper, but sanding materials specifically made for drywall are more effective. (The problem with regular sandpaper is that the fine, dusty, white powder quickly fills up the grit of the paper, wearing out the paper.) Drywall-specific sanding materials usually come precut to fit the sanding tools.

Drywall sandpaper, which has a paper back and a black carbide-grit surface, is available in 80, 100, 120 and 150 grit. The higher the grit number, the finer the sandpaper (and the smoother the finish). The 150 grit provides the smoothest finish, but it takes longer to sand down high areas or ridges. A good universal sandpaper is the 120 grit. The only time,

Sanding screen (left) and carbide sandpaper can be purchased precut to fit pole and hand sanders.

I would use the 80 or 100 grit is to rough-sand between second and third coats of joint compound (see Chapter 4).

Sanding screens, sometimes referred to as sanding cloths, are an alternative to sandpaper. The screen is a carbide-grit-coated fiberglass mesh. Both sides are coated, so when one side gets dull the screen can be turned over and used again. Because of the holes in the screen, dust buildup is seldom a problem.

Sanding screens are available in grits from 120 to 200. The 120 grit is a good all-round screen; 150 or finer grits work well for finish sanding. Sanding screens are usually more expensive than sandpaper, but you get almost twice as much life out of them. Also, a screen cuts through joint compound faster than sandpaper.

HANGING DRYWALL

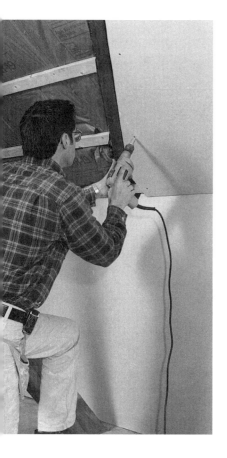

Hanging drywall has the reputation of being a difficult, strenuous job and, if done improperly, it certainly can be. But with the right attitude and the right techniques, it's not a job you need approach with trepidation. Hanging drywall can be as simple a job as covering a short partition wall or as difficult as hanging a 24-ft.-high cathedral ceiling. However big the job, hanging drywall is more than just cutting a panel and nailing it in place. Joints have to fit properly and be kept to a minimum. Holes for electrical boxes and other openings have to be cut out accurately. Fasteners have to be properly placed and properly set.

A good hanging job is the foundation for a quality taping job. When I hear someone hanging drywall say that there's no need to be fussy because the tapers can fix it, I know that the finished job will suffer. A good hanger understands the taping process and has respect for the taper.

Drywall panels can be attached in a single layer or in multiple layers. In this chapter, I'll deal with single-layer applications, though most of the procedures are the same for hanging two or more layers. Multi-layer applications will be discussed in detail in Chapter 6.

BACKING MATERIALS

For a quality finish, drywall has to be attached to a flat stable surface. There's not much structural strength in drywall, so if the framing or backing is of poor quality or weak, the drywall will probably crack or come loose. Drywall can be attached over most surfaces, but it's most commonly applied over wood or metal framing (see the sidebar on p. 54).

Wood framing

When installing drywall over wood framing, check to make sure that the framing members are aligned in a straight plane. A visual inspection is usually enough to detect badly bowed or twisted studs, though you can hold a straightedge across the studs if you prefer. If a framing member is bowed or twisted more than ¼ in., it should be replaced or straightened. Renailing will sometimes straighten out twisted framing. A bowed ceiling joist may have to be replaced, but a bowed stud can be straightened by sawing a partial kerf from the concave side. Drive a wedge into the kerfed side, and then nail a 2-ft. or longer stud alongside the existing stud to strengthen it and keep it straight (see the drawing on the facing page). Wavy or irregular ceilings can be straightened with 1x3 furring strips nailed across the joists (see p. 53). Make minor adjustments with shims driven between the joists and the furring.

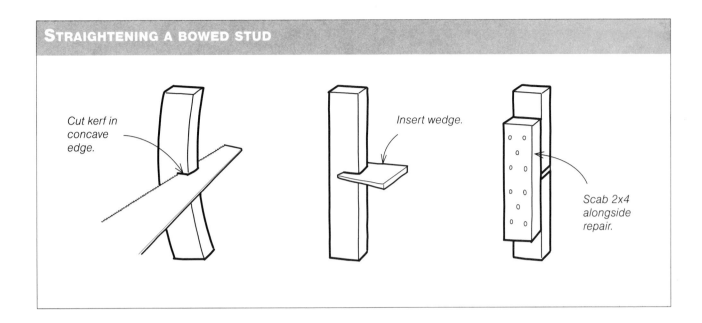

Cut kerf in concave edge.

Insert wedge.

Scab 2x4 alongside repair.

It's also important that the framing lumber be dry. If you're working in a cold climate, make sure the framing has been heated long enough to get the dampness out of the wood. I learned the lesson the hard way on a house in upstate New York that I drywalled and taped early one spring. The owners were very anxious to move in, so we were encouraged to get the job done in a hurry. Most of the house had been framed in the winter and had been exposed to a lot of snow and rain. When I started hanging drywall in the spring, it was getting warmer and the house looked dry. I brought in propane heaters to help keep the temperature above 55°F at night in preparation for taping. Everything went well, and the house looked fine when we finished. Later that summer, I got a call from a very irate owner, complaining about cracks and buckles in the drywall and peeling tape. As the lumber in the house had dried out, it shrank, twisted and settled. As the framing settled, the drywall buckled and cracked.

Solid backing

On remodeling jobs, I often attach the drywall directly over old plaster or paneling. If you're drywalling over a solid backing, be sure to use long enough fasteners to provide a firm attachment to the framing. Drywall can also be hung over rigid urethane insulation. On ceilings with rigid insulation, add 1x3 furring strips before attaching the drywall. From experience, I know that the insulation can expand just a little over time, especially with the high temperatures common in the attic or ceiling cavities. Expansion of the insulation will cause the fasteners to dimple slightly—they'll probably still be tight, but they will need to be retaped.

MEASURING AND CUTTING DRYWALL

Once you're sure that the backing material is sound, you can begin taking some measurements for the first sheet of drywall. When measuring a wall or ceiling to get a length before cutting a drywall panel, I usually take two measurements—one at approximately where each edge of the panel will be. If the

Use a 24-in. framing square to check corners for square.

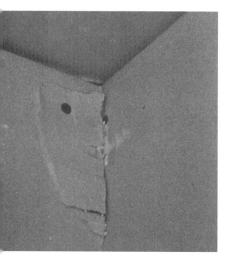

Cutting a panel to fit too tightly can cause the end to break apart. The broken section should be cut back with a utility knife.

panel that is already hung. Never cut the length so that the panel is tight and has to be forced into place. The ends will break apart and will need to be repaired when taping. Angled walls, such as gable-end walls, require careful measurements and cuts (see p. 58).

Cutting panels

Cutting drywall is probably the easiest part of the whole job. All cuts made with a utility knife are done in a similar manner, using the "score and snap" method (see the photos on the facing page). Run the utility knife along the edge to be cut, using enough pressure to cut through the paper and just into the gypsum core. One pass of the knife should be sufficient, as long as you're using a sharp blade. Snap the panel back away from the cut, and then cut the back paper with the knife. Snap the panel forward to separate the two pieces.

When cutting with a utility knife, it really doesn't matter whether you cut the face side of the panel first or the back side. I would prefer to score each panel on the face side first, but since the panels are packaged face-to-face in twos, every other panel would be facing the wrong way. The important thing to remember when cutting from the back side is to be careful not to tear the face paper on the second cut. And always snap the panel back for a clean cut. If the cut is a little ragged or you've cut the panel a little long, use a drywall rasp for smoothing and light shaping.

When cutting drywall with a drywall utility saw or a drywall saw (see p. 24), always cut from the face side of the panel to avoid damage to the finish paper as the blade is pushed through. The saw cuts on the forward stroke, but you have to be careful as you pull the

measurements are close, I'll usually use the smaller measurement. If there's quite a difference, say $5/8$ in. or more, I'll use both measurements and cut the panel out of square on one or both ends. If the panel has to be cut out of square, you have to figure out which end to cut. Check for square by placing a 24-in. framing square in each corner, as shown in the photo above.

Drywall panels should be cut to length so that they fit loosely into place. A good rule of thumb is to cut the panels about $1/4$ in. short. On ceilings, just divide the $1/4$ in. up on each end. On walls, always keep the panel edge tight against the

Whether they are straight or at an angle, all cuts across a drywall panel are made in the same way: by scoring the line of cut on the front (top), snapping the panel back and cutting along the crease on the back (middle), and snapping forward to separate the pieces (bottom).

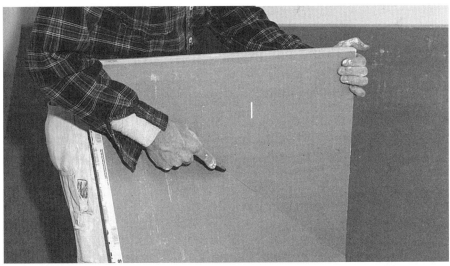

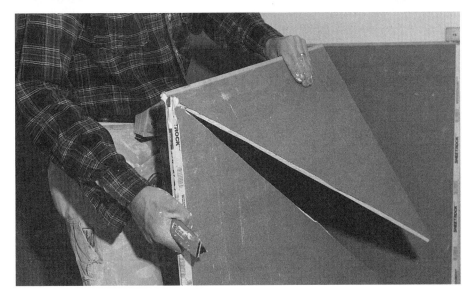

saw back not to rip the face paper. (The saw teeth will damage the back paper slightly on the forward stroke, but this is not a cause for concern.)

Cutting holes for large openings

If doors and windows are not yet installed, you can hang the drywall right over the openings before cutting them out. With the panel installed, cut along each side of the opening with a drywall saw. Score along the top of the opening on the back side of the panel, snap forward and cut off the waste with a utility knife.

If the doors and windows have already been installed, you'll have to measure and cut out the opening before hanging the drywall. Mark the opening on the face side of the panel and cut out with a drywall saw. If the window is installed, but not the window jambs, the panel can be attached before the opening is cut out. Just follow each side of the window's rough opening with a saw. The top of the window opening can also be cut with a saw, but it's easier to score the height of the window opening on the back side of the panel with a utility knife before it is attached. Scoring the back first allows you to snap the waste piece forward and cut along the face side after the panel is hung and the sides are cut (see the photo below).

Cutting holes for small openings

Cutting out holes for electrical-outlet boxes, switches and other small openings is trickier than making continuous straight cuts, but with a little practice and some careful measuring it's really not that hard to master. There are a few different ways to mark and cut the openings, but the main distinction is whether you make the cuts before you hang the panel or after.

To cut the opening before hanging the panel, you first have to measure the box's coordinates and then transfer them to the panel. The problem with this method is that the box never seems to line up perfectly with the cut opening. This misalignment is because the wall, floor or attached panel you're measuring from probably isn't perfectly square or level or gaps may not have been accounted for. Even if everything is square, it's still pretty easy to make a mistake with this method. Some outlet covers and fixtures barely cover a $\frac{1}{4}$-in. area around the box, so being precise is important in order to avoid having to patch (see p. 113).

Another method you can use on walls is to rub the face of the outlet box with chalk and then press the panel against it. The chalk leaves an outline of the box on the back of the panel.

Because of the potential for error with the "cut-first" method, I prefer to cut boxes out after the drywall is tacked in

If the window trim has not been installed, you can drywall right over the window and then cut out the opening.

To mark an opening for an outlet box, first use a framing square to mark the sides and the height of the box from the floor (left). Tack the panel in place, and then transfer the measurements to the face of the panel (right).

place. It's not only more accurate but also faster. Notice that I said "tacked in place"—use only enough fasteners so that the panel will not fall, and don't nail or screw to the stud or joist that the box is attached to. Fastening too close to the box could put pressure on the box and cause the drywall to break apart when you make the cut (see the photo at left on p. 56).

One way to mark a square or rectangular opening is to use a framing square to transfer the location of the sides of the opening to the drywall. Mark the exact location of each side of the opening on the floor and write down the height of the top and bottom (see the photo at left above). After tacking the panel in place, transfer the measurements to the panel using the square (see the photo at right above), and then cut out the open-

ing carefully with a utility saw. Bear in mind that the box usually sticks out past the framing the thickness of the drywall, so you have to cut around the *outside* of the box.

Round boxes on walls or ceilings can be cut out just as easily, though the method of marking the location is just a little different (see the sidebar on p. 46).

An alternative to cutting out electrical boxes with a utility saw is to use an electric drywall router (see the photo at left on p. 47). Before routing an outlet box, first make sure that the power is off and that the electrical wires are pushed far enough into the box so that the router bit will not reach them. (The router bit should stick out of the router only about ¼ in. more than the thickness of the drywall being cut.) Next, measure from

The most accurate way to cut out an opening for a round fixture box is to measure the box's coordinates, tack the drywall panel in place, transfer the measurements to the panel and then make the cut.

To mark the location of the fixture box, first measure the height of the top and bottom, then the left and right sides. Write these measurements down.

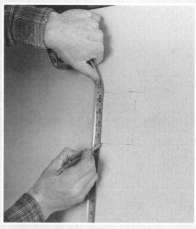

Tack the panel in place, and then transfer the measurements to the panel face.

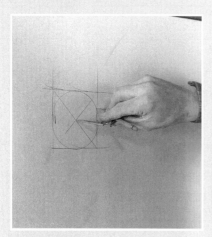

Locate the center of the opening by drawing diagonal lines, and use a scriber to draw the circle.

Gently cut around the outside edges of the box with a utility saw.

The cut panel fits snugly around the box.

the center of the box to the nearest wall or floor and make a mark. Tack the panel in place, and locate the center of the box. With the router running, push the bit through the panel and gently move it to one side until you feel it hit the side of the box. Now pull the bit out and hop it over to the outside of the box. Keep light pressure against the box and push the router around it in a counterclockwise direction.

You can also use the router for cutting out larger openings, such as for heat ducts and vents. The tool takes a little getting used to, but it does a nice clean job—and it's fast. The only drawback with using a router is that it generates a lot of fine dust, so I'd recommend wearing an approved dust mask if you opt for this method.

GENERAL GUIDELINES FOR HANGING DRYWALL

A properly planned drywall-hanging job is a team effort, and within the team each person should have specific responsibilities. When drywalling an entire house, my crew and I start by hanging all the large ceilings. With three crew members, two can measure, cut and lift the panels into position, and the third can screw the panels down and cut out any electrical boxes. Once the ceilings are attached, we usually follow the same procedure for the walls, hanging all the larger panels as a team first and then splitting up to fit and hang all the smaller pieces individually.

It would be difficult for one person working alone to hang an 8-ft. piece of drywall on a ceiling or even on the

A drywall router is a speedy alternative to a utility saw for cutting out an opening in a drywall panel.

CARRYING DRYWALL

Carrying a drywall panel is a two-person job. Both carriers should be on the same side of the panel, with the same hand under the bottom edge and the other hand steadying the top. They should hold the panel a foot or more in from each end and let the panel lean against their shoulders. Working together in this way is the least strenuous way to carry drywall.

upper part of a wall without help. Getting enough help is important, especially since it's preferable to hang longer lengths of drywall. Use panels that span the entire length of a wall or ceiling whenever possible. If one panel won't cover the length, still use long panels to avoid having too many butted seams.

And always stagger butted seams away from each other and away from the center of a wall or ceiling.

FASTENING DRYWALL

The preferred method for attaching drywall over wood or metal framing is with drywall screws. Screws are inserted with a drywall screwgun so that the screwhead sits just below the surface of the panel without breaking the face paper (see the photo at far left). With the screwgun set to the correct depth adjustment, the screw pulls the panel tight against the framing; when the screw stops turning, the clutch disengages. The screwhead spins the paper as it sinks in, leaving a slight dimple and a clean smooth edge around the screw head. Make sure to hold the screwgun firmly, as shown in the photo at left, and insert the screw straight in (a screw that's even slightly tilted will not set deep enough and may tear the face paper). Space the screws evenly on each framing member according to the specifications in the chart below. Place screws at least 3/8 in. from the edge of the panel to avoid damage to the edge.

The screwhead at left has been sunk too deep, tearing the face paper around it. The screw at right is set correctly.

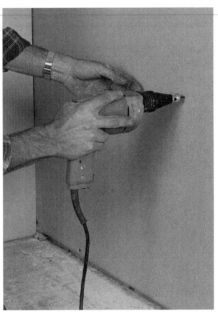

Hold the screwgun firmly as you drive a screw so that your entire hand and forearm absorb most of the stress.

If you are going to use nails instead of drywall screws, make sure to use ring-shank nails specified for attaching drywall to wood framing. As with screws, keep nails at least 3/8 in. from the edges and follow the same spacing schedule. When the ends of the panels butt against each other, nail approximately every 8 in. on either side of the joint.

One difference when using nails instead of screws is that all nails "in the field" (across the face of the panel) should be double-nailed. Begin nailing at one edge and work toward the opposite edge. To help keep the drywall tight against the framing, apply hand pressure on the panel next to the nail as you drive it in. Set one nail lightly and then set another

FASTENER SPACING		
Framing Type	Framing Spacing	Maximum Fastener Spacing
Ceiling joists	16 in. o.c.	12 in.
	24 in. o.c.	10 in.
Wall studs	16 in. o.c.	16 in.
	24 in. o.c.	16 in.

nail 1½ in. to 2 in. away. Gently hit each nail until it is firmly set in a shallow, uniform dimple formed by the last blow of the drywall hammer. Do not break the paper, and keep damage to the gypsum core in the dimpled area to a minimum.

If you use nails, I recommend that you do so only along the edges of the panel, and then fill in with drywall screws in the field. My usual way of working is to tack the panels in place along the edges with nails and then finish the attachment with screws. I want to get the panel up as quickly as possible, and it's faster to use nails than screws. Once the panel is tacked in place, I cut out all the openings, and then screw the centers and any spots missed along the edges. I prefer to use screws rather than nails along butted seams for a more stable joint.

When nailing or screwing along the bottom of a panel or along the edge of a doorway or a window, place fasteners as close to the panel edge as possible (but no closer than ⅜ in.). The trim will cover these fasteners, which means a few less screws or nails to tape.

Adhesive technique

Whether you use screws or nails, it takes a lot of fasteners to attach all the panels on a ceiling or wall. One way to cut down on the number of fasteners needed (and to eliminate the problem of fastener pops and loose panels) is to secure the drywall with adhesive. (Another fastener-saving method is to use the "floating-corners" technique, as explained in the sidebar on p. 53.)

Using an adhesive (which should be approved for wood-to-drywall application) reduces the number of fasteners required by up to 75%. It also adds strength to the structure. Apply a ⅜-in.-wide bead of adhesive to each framing member to within 6 in. of the edges of the drywall. Wherever the panels butt

Space screws about 12 in. apart across the face of a ceiling panel.

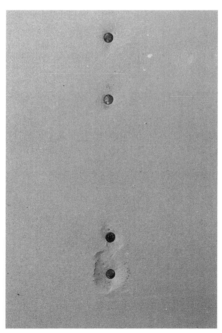

Nails should be set in a shallow dimple (top), not hammered so deep that they break the paper and damage the gypsum core (bottom).

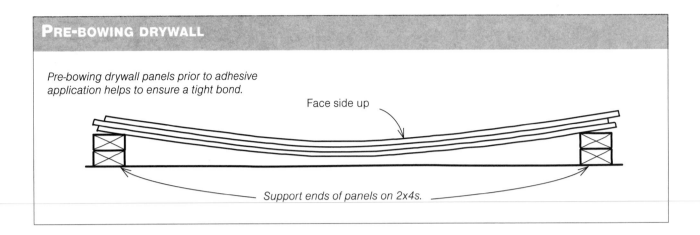

Pre-bowing drywall panels prior to adhesive application helps to ensure a tight bond.

Face side up

Support ends of panels on 2x4s.

together, apply a bead of adhesive to each edge of the framing member. Install fasteners along the perimeter of each panel immediately after it is hung.

On panels attached horizontally on walls, no face nailing or screwing is necessary, except on butted seams and then only enough to form a flush finish (every 10 in. to 12 in.). If the panels are attached vertically, the face should be screwed into each stud at 24-in. centers. For ceilings, install one screw every 24 in. (the screw can be removed after 24 hours to cut down on the number of fasteners).

When using adhesive to attach drywall, it's helpful to pre-bow the panels before you hang them. Stack the panels face side up overnight, with the ends supported on 2x4s (see the drawing above). When the pre-bowed panel is fastened around the perimeter, the center is forced tight against the adhesive on the framing, thereby eliminating the need for any temporary fasteners. Allow the adhesive to dry for at least 48 hours before starting the taping process. (Note that the adhesive method of attachment will not work over a plastic vapor barrier or over insulation where the kraft paper overlaps the framing.)

HANGING CEILINGS

In a room that's going to be drywalled on the ceiling and on the walls, always attach the ceiling panels first. By hanging the ceiling first, the ceiling panels can be cut so that they slip easily into place, and the wall panels will fit against the ceiling to help support the edges.

I usually use adjustable step-up benches to hang ceilings 9 ft. high or less. Center the benches under the section to be hung and lift one end of the panel into position. Keep the other end low, and then push it up into position as your co-worker holds the higher end in place (see the top photo on the facing page). Once in place, the panel can be held against the framing by applying gentle pressure with the top of your head while you fasten it. Alternatively, you can use a T-support to hold the panel in place (see the photo on p. 25).

I know a few drywall hangers who use stilts when hanging drywall. One crew member on the floor does the cutting and hands the panel to two other crew members on stilts. They in turn lift the panel into place on the ceiling and attach it, cut openings for any electrical boxes and take the next measurement. Under ideal conditions, working from stilts can be the fastest way to hang dry-

Ceilings should always be hung before the walls. Keep one end of the panel low while you position the other end.

Support the panel with gentle head pressure as you prepare to tack it in place.

GRAIN ORIENTATION IN DRYWALL

In Chapter 1, I listed the maximum on-center spacing of framing for the various types and thicknesses of drywall. In many instances, the framing has to be closer if ceiling panels are hung parallel to the joists. I've known this to be true since I started drywalling, but I never really gave too much thought as to why. After reading an article about grain orientation in drywall in *Fine Homebuilding* magazine (#98), I now understand why.

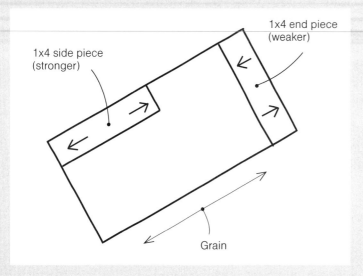

1x4 end piece (weaker)

1x4 side piece (stronger)

Grain

Arden VanNorman performed a simple test to prove that drywall is stronger "with the grain" than across it. He cut one 1x4 piece from the end of a panel and one from the side, as shown in the drawing above.

Stacking bricks in the middle of each piece quickly shows that the end piece is much weaker than the side piece. Accordingly, drywall hung perpendicular to the framing members is stronger than drywall hung parallel.

A simple test proves that drywall is stronger with the grain than across it.

wall on ceilings, but I prefer not to use them for this job. The two crew members on stilts really can't help with the cutting and carrying of panels, which means a lot of work for the person on the floor. In addition, the work area has to be kept clean and uncluttered to minimize the risk of falls.

Ceiling panels can be hung perpendicular to the joists or parallel to the joists. For a number of reasons, I prefer to attach the ceiling panels perpendicular to the joists:

• Drywall is less likely to sag if hung in this direction (as explained in the sidebar at left).

• Butted seams can be attached to a solid nailer for the length of the seam.

• It's easier to see the joists when fastening the panels.

• If the on-center spacing of a ceiling joist is off, it won't matter that much and may not even be noticed.

• The drywall will float over slightly uneven joists and make them less conspicuous.

The only reason I'd hang drywall parallel to the joists would be to avoid butted seams on the ceiling. Before opting for this method, check the spacing of the joists carefully—they have to be spaced so that the edge of each panel falls on the center of a joist. If the tapered edges don't hit on center, you may have to cut the long edge of the panel to correct it, which would create a long butted seam. Also be careful not to put a seam on a joist that is either crowned up or sagged down, which would be a difficult seam to hide when taping.

If butted seams cannot be avoided, no matter in which direction the panels are hung, stagger the butted seams and

The inside corners where wall meets wall or ceiling meets wall are prone to cracking and fastener pops caused by stress at the intersection. One way to reduce fastener problems is to eliminate fasteners at one or both edges in the corners. I call this the "floating-corners" technique.

On ceilings, place the first screw about 7 in. from the ceiling edge along the perimeter of the ceiling. When the top panel of the wall is pushed up against the ceiling, it will support the edges of the ceiling panels. Screw the upper edge of the top wall panel in place about 8 in. down from the ceiling.

For the vertical corners on wall panels, omit fasteners on the first panel installed in the corner (see the drawing at right). Fastening the abutting panel in the corner helps support the first panel installed. Follow this method for the entire height of the wall corner. Screw or nail the remaining ceiling and wall areas using standard fastening procedures.

By eliminating the fasteners in the corners, the drywall is still held firmly in place, but if the corner framing flexes or settles a little the corners will most likely be unaffected. (Note that the corners that are not fastened still need to have standard wood framing behind them.)

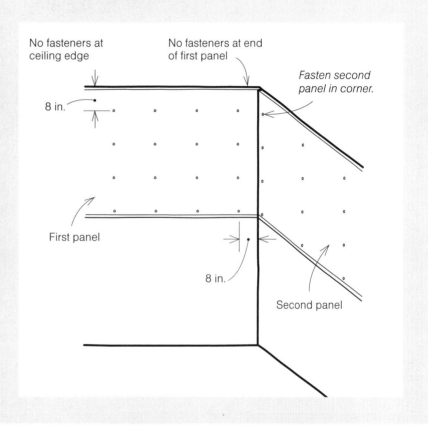

No fasteners at ceiling edge

No fasteners at end of first panel

Fasten second panel in corner.

8 in.

First panel

8 in.

Second panel

keep them as far away from the center of the ceilings as possible. Butted seams are easier to conceal if they are kept away from each other, and discontinuous butted seams are also less likely to crack. (For more on butted seams, see Chapter 6.)

Some ceilings are furred with 1x3s perpendicular to the joists before the drywall is hung. A ceiling may be furred

for a number of reasons: to help straighten out a wavy ceiling, to decrease the distance between nailers (ceiling joists), or to provide solid nailing over rigid insulation. The 3-in. wide face makes an excellent target when fastening the drywall. The 1x3 furring strip should be treated just like a ceiling joist, and the drywall should be hung following the same procedures.

One final note: When hanging a cathedral ceiling, it's easier to attach the lower panel first, and then work your way up to the top. By starting at the bottom, you'll have an edge for the panel to rest on when you hang the next run, which is easier than trying to lift the panel up to fit against the panel above.

HANGING WALLS

Once you've attached all the ceilings, it's time to start working on the walls. Walls are usually a lot easier to hang than ceilings—you may have to make more cuts for electrical boxes and other openings on a wall, but at least you're not working over your head. Before hanging the walls, it's a good idea to mark the location of the wall studs on the ceiling and floor to make it easier to locate studs once they are covered. Mark the location of any electrical boxes or other openings that will be cut out after the drywall is attached, too (see pp. 44-47).

As with ceilings, you can hang the wall panels in two ways—in this case, horizontally or vertically. In most cases, for

ATTACHING DRYWALL TO METAL FRAMING

Drywall can be hung on metal framing in much the same way as on wood framing, but there are a couple of things to watch out for.

Metal studs and joists are made out of a thin piece of steel bent into a C-shaped stud. Before attaching drywall to the metal studs, check to see which direction the open side of the stud faces (they should all be installed in the same direction). On a long wall that is going to have butted seams, the drywall should be attached from the end that the open side of the stud faces (see the drawing below).

For the seams to end up flat, the drywall must be attached in the proper sequence. Fasten the edge of the first panel to the unsupported open edge of the stud. Screw on the entire length before attaching the abutting panel.

If the panel were attached to the solid side first and then to the unsupported side, the screw might deflect the open end and force the panel edges out. When screwing on the rest of the panel, keep the screws closer to the solid edge of the stud. (Note that you should always use screws, not nails, when fastening drywall to metal framing.)

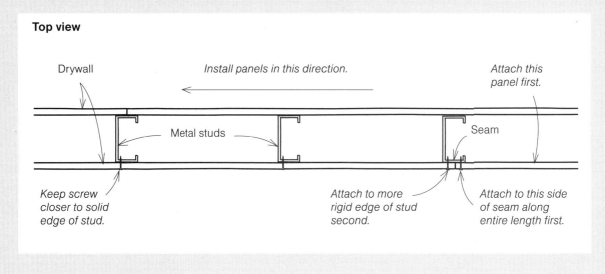

Top view

Drywall

Install panels in this direction.

Attach this panel first.

Metal studs

Seam

Keep screw closer to solid edge of stud.

Attach to more rigid edge of stud second.

Attach to this side of seam along entire length first.

Start nails on the top panel before lifting it into place.

walls 8 ft. high or less (or 9 ft. high if I'm using 54-in. panels), I prefer to hang the drywall horizontally. Here's why:

• Standing drywall on end increases the linear footage of seams that have to be taped by up to 25% (see the drawing on p. 12).

• Horizontal application of drywall gives extra bracing strength because it ties more studs together.

• Seams are easier to hide because light usually shines along the finished seams, which makes them less obvious. A seam going against the studs just flows over any studs that may not be perfectly straight, which helps hide these imperfections.

• Seams are easier to tape because they are at a convenient working height.

Hang the top panel first, fitting it tightly against the ceiling. If the wall to be hung has a window opening, cut the panel to length first and then score the

Lift the panel up against the ceiling and nail in place.

back side with a utility knife at the location of the top of the window opening (see p. 44). Now stand the panel on the floor exactly below where it will be attached, leaning it against the studs. Start a nail about 1 in. down, lining it up with each stud. Lift the panel up against the ceiling and drive the nails home.

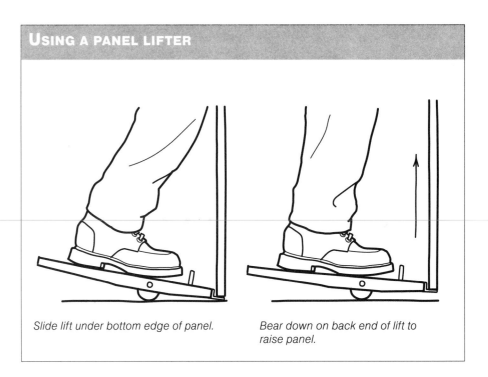

Slide lift under bottom edge of panel.

Bear down on back end of lift to raise panel.

Putting too much pressure on the panel with your foot as you cut an opening for an electrical box can break the face of the panel.

Run panels long at doorways and outside corners, and then cut off the excess after the panels are attached.

Once the top of the panel is nailed in place, cut out any small openings, and then finish fastening the panel and cut out any window or door openings. Next cut the bottom panel to fit against the top panel. The panel should be about ½ in. short in height, so it will not fit tight against the floor and bust apart when fastened into place. Cutting it a little short also leaves room for a panel lifter or a prybar to be slid under the panel so it can be raised into place (see the drawing on the facing page).

Most of the electrical outlets are located near the floor, so just tack the top of the panel and then cut out the electrical boxes (as explained on pp. 44-47). Remember not to put too much pressure on the panel, which could cause the face to break apart around the box (see the photo at bottom left on the facing page).

As on the ceiling, any butted seams should be staggered and placed away from the center of the wall. Butted seams can also be located above doors and above or below windows. Placing butted joints in these areas will create a shorter seam, since part of the seam would fall in the opening. Try to keep the seam at least 8 in. in from the edge of the opening because the wall is more stable away from the edge. Also, the slight crown formed when taping could affect the trim miter joint if the seam is located at the corner.

When hanging panels on an outside corner, run the panels long and trim them off after they're attached (you can use the same technique on the bottom panel adjoining a door opening). Running the panel long means one less measurement and also allows some flexibility if inside corners are not plumb and have to be scribed to fit. And if the framing isn't square or plumb at the outside corner, the panel can be cut to fit the exact angle so there will be no big gaps under the corner bead.

SUMMARY FOR HANGING DRYWALL

- **Always hang ceilings first.**
- **Don't cut panels so that they fit too tightly, and never force panels into place.**
- **Place tapered edges together whenever possible.**
- **Try to hang panels so that they are perpendicular to the framing.**
- **Try to span the length of a wall or ceiling with one panel.**
- **Stagger butted seams away from each other and away from the center of a wall or ceiling.**
- **When hanging a cathedral ceiling, start at the bottom edge of the ceiling.**
- **Cut out electrical boxes and other small openings after the panels are tacked in place.**
- **Use screws rather than nails (and screws only with metal framing).**
- **Fasten close to the edges of doorways and windows and along the floor to avoid having to tape these fasteners.**
- **Attach metal corner bead to all outside corners, uncased openings, beams and soffits.**

HANGING A GARAGE

Garages, which are typically large rooms with high ceilings, require a somewhat different hanging strategy than most rooms within the house.

The ceilings are usually too large to cover without butted seams, so I almost always hang the drywall perpendicular to the joists.

If the ceiling is over 9 ft. high, I'll often hang the garage walls parallel to the studs—that is, vertically rather than horizontally. By standing the panels on end, I can avoid any butted seams on the walls and not add too much to the linear footage of seams. If you hang wall panels vertically, just make sure to check that the studs are reasonably straight and on center.

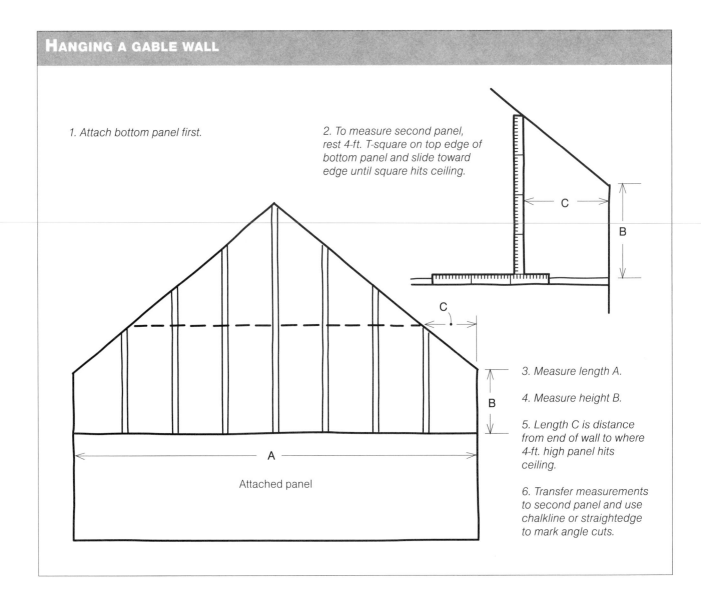

1. Attach bottom panel first.

2. To measure second panel, rest 4-ft. T-square on top edge of bottom panel and slide toward edge until square hits ceiling.

Attached panel

3. Measure length A.

4. Measure height B.

5. Length C is distance from end of wall to where 4-ft. high panel hits ceiling.

6. Transfer measurements to second panel and use chalkline or straightedge to mark angle cuts.

Gable walls For gable ends of a room with a cathedral or sloped ceiling, I usually hang the bottom panel first (see the drawing above). The floor is a good flat surface to measure from, and the bottom panel usually has a square end for at least part of the height. The second panel can be measured from the bottom panel. Setting the panels on top of each other helps make it easier to hold them in place, especially when the ceiling is high. Note that you should not locate or fasten a butted seam on the center support of the gable end. The building might move or settle at this point causing stress to the drywall.

Corner protection

After the drywall has been attached, all outside corners, uncased openings, beams and soffits should be protected with metal corner beads. The corner beads resist impact and form a straight raised edge for taping. Where possible, corner beads should be installed in one piece; if the corner's too long, beads should be butted together, not over-lapped. Make sure that the butted edges are even with each other and straight.

Attach corner bead with a corner crimper (see p. 30) or with screws (or with nails if drywalling over wood framing). If you use a crimper, crimp the corner every 4 in. to 6 in. If screwing or nailing, fasten every 8 in. to 10 in. and 1 in. from the top and bottom.

For ceiling-to-floor corner beads, cut the corner bead with tin snips about ½ in. short and push it tight against the ceil-ing. Leaving the corner bead a little short eliminates the risk of the bead binding and coming loose or cracking if the wall settles. The baseboard will cover the gap along the floor. Fasten from the top down, driving the screws or nails in opposite each other, making sure the edges of the bead lie flat against the wall. If the edges do not hug the wall tightly, use more fasteners. The edge should not stick out past the raised bead on the outside corner edge.

The final stage in hanging the drywall is to install metal corner beads at all outside corners, uncased openings, beams and soffits.

4

TAPING

For me, taping over freshly hung drywall is the most enjoyable part of a drywalling job. It's fast-paced work that's not too demanding physically, and it's pretty much dust-free, which is a nice break after the hanging stage. Taping is also the part of the drywalling process that requires the most skill and the most patience. As you'll see in this chapter, there's more to taping than just concealing the joints between panels—a properly taped joint should be as strong and durable as the drywall panel itself.

Some drywallers use mechanical taping tools (such as a "banjo," a tool that applies joint tape and compound at the same time), but I prefer to do all my taping by hand. In this chapter I'll take you through the steps of taping done with hand tools (discussed in Chapter 2) and also describe some common taping problems, and ways to avoid and correct them.

TAPING BASICS

Drywall is typically finished, or "taped," with three coats of joint compound and then lightly sanded to produce a smooth surface suitable for decorating with most types of paints, textures or wall coverings. Three coats of joint compound are necessary to conceal the joints, corners and fasteners. In some cases (when applying a setting-type compound, for example), you can get

acceptable results with just two coats, but three coats will help ensure a more professional-looking job.

The first coat, which is commonly called the tape-embedding coat or rough coat, does not have to be perfect. It just has to be neat and of consistent thickness and width. The second coat is a filler coat, during which the joint tape used between panels is hidden and the edges of the joint compound are feathered out. The third coat, often referred to as the finish coat, is a thin layer of compound applied lightly over the second coat to smooth out any remaining rough areas. Each coat is applied a little wider than the previous coat, and the edges are feathered out to leave a smooth surface.

What should be taped?

Joint compound alone has little strength, and if a joint between panels were just filled with compound, the joint would inevitably crack. To strengthen the joint, paper or fiberglass-mesh tape has to be used with the compound. The compound acts like an adhesive, but it's the tape that actually joins the two panels together. With the tape centered on the joint and embedded in the joint compound, the face paper of the two panels essentially becomes one solid surface. The layers of the joint compound that cover the tape are used to conceal the joint.

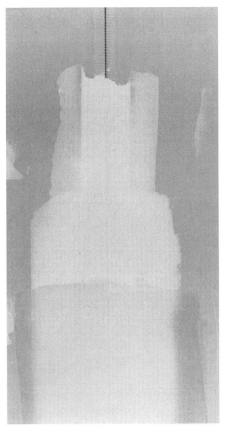

Joints between drywall panels are covered with fiberglass-mesh or paper tape, and then coated with three layers of joint compound.

All fasteners, joints between panels, and inside and outside corners require taping.

The same principle applies for cracks, holes and hammer marks that tear the surface of the drywall: They all need to be covered with paper or mesh tape to strengthen the surface. Inside corners on walls and ceilings are also joints that need to be strengthened as well as concealed. Paper tape is embedded in the corner and, after it dries, covered with two or more coats of joint compound. Fasteners, dents or slight imperfections can be concealed with joint compound alone. Since the surface is unbroken, the area is still strong and tape is unnecessary.

What to expect when taping

Taping requires patience as well as skill. If I apply the first coat of tape and compound on Monday, I'll wait until Tuesday when the first coat is fully dry before going over everything again with the second coat. On Wednesday, I'll apply the third coat. As each coat of joint compound is applied, I have to become more particular, smoothing out the compound to blend in with the surface of the drywall.

The time it takes to finish taping a certain square footage of drywall is affected by many different circumstances, including the height of the ceiling, the number of joints and corners, the quality of the hanging job, and the temperature and

Any damaged areas at inside corners (or anywhere else) should be filled with a coat of compound before you begin the first coat.

humidity on the job site. I usually figure on taking the same amount of time for each coat: If it takes 8 hours to apply the first coat, it will take about 8 hours for the second coat and another 8 hours for the third.

Taping can be a messy job, and it would be very difficult to avoid getting joint compound on your hands, your clothes and the floor. I keep an old taping knife and an empty pail handy so I can scoop up dropped joint compound before it gets walked on. The work area should be clean and uncluttered so that the walls and ceilings can be finished along their entire length, without having to worry about tripping or falling (this is especially important if you're working on stilts). Having to move tools, drywall scraps or building materials from place to place every time you tape can waste a lot of time and lead to frustration and loss of concentration.

Before you begin

Before you start taping, make sure that all the drywall panels are firmly attached, that all the electrical outlet boxes and other openings have been cut out and that corner bead has been installed where necessary. The temperature of the air, joint compound and drywall surface should be consistent, and at least 55°F if you're using drying types of joint compound and 45°F if using setting types. Ideally, the temperature should be 65°F to 70°F. Good ventilation and low humidity also help the joint compound dry and set up properly.

If there are any damaged areas of drywall, such as busted-out inside corners or outlet-box openings, cut away the loose drywall and fill with a thin coat of joint compound. Also fill any gaps between panels that are over ¼ in. wide. Allow these areas to dry before applying the first coat. If time is of the essence, use the setting-type compound as a filler (see pp. 36-37).

Mixing joint compound

As explained in Chapter 2, joint compounds are available in powdered form and ready-mixed. I mix powdered compounds (either setting type or drying type) with water in a 5-gal. joint-compound pail, using a heavy-duty ½-in. electric drill with a mixing paddle (see the top photo on the facing page).

Setting-type compound If you're mixing a setting-type compound, it's especially important to make sure that the pail and mixing paddle are clean, since even a thin film of dry compound on either one can cause the compound to set up prematurely. The hardened compound can also come loose and get mixed in, leaving chunks in the mixed compound.

Follow the directions on the bag concerning the proportions of water and compound. Pour the specified amount of cool (not cold or hot) water into the pail, and then add the compound. Mix until the compound reaches the desired consistency: It should be stiff enough to hold its form on the trowel (see the bottom photo on the facing page), but not so stiff that it is difficult to smooth out. Be careful not to overmix, because too much mixing can shorten the hardening time. It's important not to mix any more compound than you can use within the time specified on the bag. Once this time has expired, the compound will harden chemically. Don't try to mix any setting-type compound that has started to set up—it's unusable.

Drying-type compound With powdered drying-type compounds, add the compound to the specified amount of water and mix well until the powder is completely damp. After 15 minutes, remix. This type of compound will not set up, so it can be kept for extended periods of time (as long as it's covered), and can be remixed if necessary.

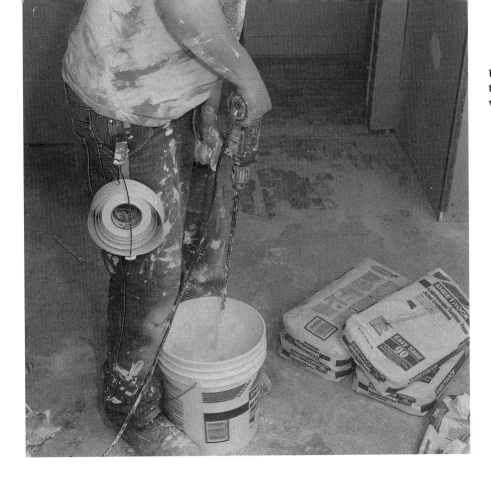

Use a powered mixing paddle to mix powdered compounds with water.

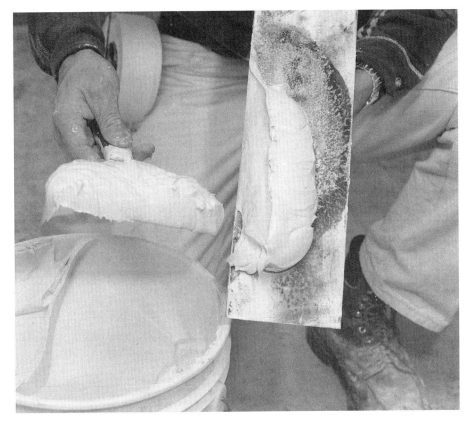

Mix the compound so that it is stiff enough to hold on the trowel without sliding off.

When loosening up ready-mixed joint compound, use a masher-type mixer to avoid mixing too much air into the joint compound.

Ready-mixed compounds are usually used at the consistency that they come in the pail, but they can be thinned for taping. I often thin the compound for the third coat. Add a little water at a time to avoid overthinning (if the compound gets too thin, you can add additional compound to attain the correct consistency). If the compound freezes, allow it to unthaw at room temperature and mix without adding water. If the compound has sat too long and separated so that a clear liquid forms on top, it can usually be remixed. If it smells sour or looks moldy, the compound has gone bad and should not be used.

FIRST COAT

I begin the first coat by filling all the fastener heads, move on to the flat, tapered edge seams (including any outside corners) and then finish with the inside corners.

Screws and nail heads

I like to tape the fastener (screw and nail) heads first so that I don't accidentally mess up a seam that I've already taped. You need only a thin layer of joint compound to conceal the fasteners, and it's easiest to tape a row of two or three fasteners in a single strip rather than individually (see the photo on the facing page). Use a 5-in. or 6-in. taping knife, applying just enough pressure to fill the indentation and leave the face of the drywall panel covered with a very thin film of compound. Don't be tempted to try and fill the indentation with one thick coat; applying three thin coats of compound and tapering the edges will bring the indentations level with the panel surface and require only minimal sanding.

Seams

The seams between the edges of drywall panels take considerably more time to first-coat than fastener heads because they require application of tape as well

Ready-mixed compound If a ready-mixed compound is fresh, no mixing is necessary, but if it has been sitting around for a while, you'll sometimes need to loosen it up by adding a little water. Even if no water needs to be added, it's a good idea to mix the compound so that it has the same consistency throughout the pail. I prefer to use a masher-type mixer rather than a powered mixing paddle for ready-mixed compounds because the electric mixer can whip air into the compound, which can cause pitting or bubbles in the taped seams (see pp. 83-85).

as joint compound. There are two ways to tape these seams: with fiberglass-mesh tape or with paper tape.

Mesh-tape method On the tapered edge seams between panels, I recommend using self-adhesive fiberglass-mesh tape (see p. 35) rather than paper tape. Mesh tape is fast and easy to use, and you don't have to worry about air bubbles under the tape or loose tape, which can be a problem when using paper tape.

On the downside, mesh tape is not as strong as paper tape, so it's important to use the right type of joint compound with it. You can embed mesh tape in any type of setting-type compound, but if you're working with drying-type compounds make sure to use a taping compound, not a topping or an all-

TAPING SEQUENCE

If you're just learning to tape, it's probably easiest to go through the house from room to room and apply the first coat to all the fastener heads first. Then go back and do all the flat seams between panels, and, when these are dry, first-coat the inside and outside corners. Working this way means that you won't have to worry about messing up a flat seam when you're working on a corner, which can be a problem if the seam is still wet.

However, doing each step separately is not a very efficient way of working. Once you've got the hang of taping, it's much faster to complete each step on each surface as you go along. For example, if I'm taping walls, I'll tape all the screws on one wall first, then the flat seams and finally the inside corners. Once one wall is complete, I'll go on to the next wall until the whole room is done.

To save time as you're taping, make sure you have all the taping tools you may need handy—in your hands or your back pocket, or by a pail of joint compound. And keep the pail of joint compound close by, moving it along with you as you tape.

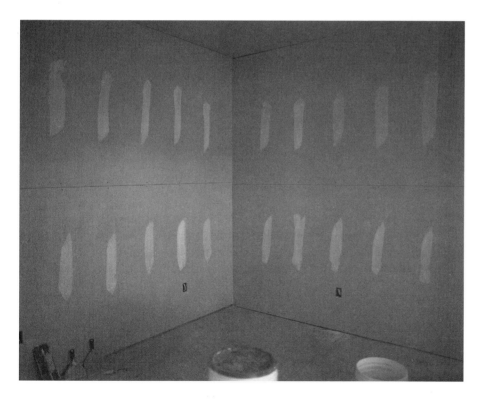

Fasteners are easier to conceal if they are taped in strips of two or three rather than individually.

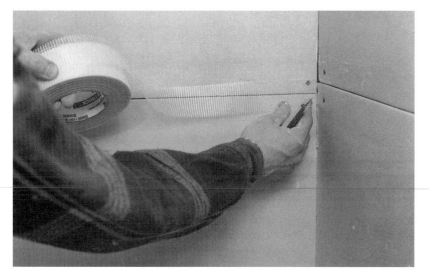

purpose compound (see p. 36). I prefer to use a setting-type compound because it's stronger and shrinks and cracks very little when drying.

When using mesh tape, I apply the tape to all the joints in the room before applying the joint compound. Press the tape firmly over the joint so that it lies flat with no wrinkles, and cut to length with a sharp taping knife or a utility knife. Using a hawk or a large (4-in. by 14-in.) beveled trowel as a palette, apply the joint compound with a 5-in. or 6-in. taping knife to the entire length of the joint. Put a small amount of compound on the taping knife and press the compound onto the center of the joint for the width of the trowel. A thin, even layer of com-

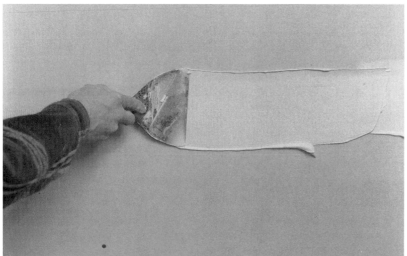

Cover the joint between the tapered edges of drywall panels with self-adhesive mesh tape, being careful to avoid wrinkles in the tape (top). Apply a thin, even layer of compound the width of the trowel over the mesh tape (center). Hold the beveled trowel almost flat against the surface of the panels and pull it along the joint to smooth the compound and feather out the edges (bottom).

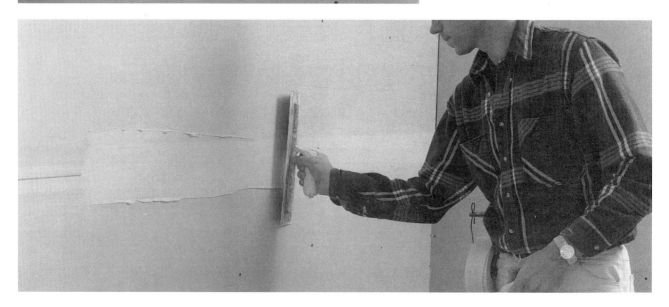

pound about 1/4 in. thick is all that you need. Don't worry about the compound being too smooth at this point.

Now switch to the 4-in. by 14-in. beveled trowel. With the trowel centered on the seam and held almost flat against the panels, pull the trowel along the joint, smoothing the compound with the back edge. Leave a layer of compound that will just cover the tape and fill the recessed area of the tapered seam. The edges should be fairly smooth and feathered out. If a lot of compound builds up in front of the trowel and pushes out around the sides as you smooth the seam, either you've put too much compound on the seam or you're taking too much off. When you've finished the seam, the joint compound should be about 3/16 in. thick in the center and 8 in. wide from one tapered edge to the other. Remember, the first coat doesn't have to be perfect—just make sure that you don't build up the compound too thickly and don't leave ridges that will make the application of the second coat more difficult.

Paper-tape method While mesh tape works fine on the tapered edge seams between panels, it's not strong enough to use on butted end seams. Butted seams need the extra strength of paper tape to reduce the risk of cracking (which is greater for butted seams because they are typically spliced on a single stud or joist). Unlike mesh tape, paper tape forms a strong joint on seams when used with *any* type of joint compound. Paper tape used in conjunction with an all-purpose joint compound is the most common way to tape seams (whether tapered edge or butted).

The procedure for embedding paper tape is somewhat different than for mesh tape. Because the paper tape is not self-adhesive, you first have to lay down a ground coat of compound to hold the paper in place (see the photos on p. 68). Use a 5-in. or 6-in. taping knife to apply a thin, fairly even layer of joint compound along the center of the seam approximately 1/4 in. thick. (Note that you can work on more than one seam at a time, but usually not on every seam in the room: The compound may start to dry before you get to the last seams, making it more difficult to work with and more likely to form air bubbles behind the paper tape.) Next, center the paper tape on the joint and press it very lightly into place. Keep the tape pulled tight and reasonably straight along the joint. Rip the tape to the desired length, making sure that the tape goes far enough into each corner so that the corner tape will overlap the joint tape.

With the paper tape in position, pull the taping knife along the center of the tape. I usually start at the center of a seam and pull toward each end. (If the joint butts into an inside corner, be careful not to leave too much compound under the tape as you approach the corner to avoid raising a bump.) Keep enough pressure on the knife so that the tape is properly embedded as you go. The pressure on the knife should push the extra compound out from the edges, leaving a layer about 1/8 in. thick under the tape. Make sure the tape is flat, wrinkle-free and tight against the panel at the tape edges. Clean excess compound from along the edges of the joint with the taping knife. As when using mesh tape, the first coat should be about 8 in. wide.

Try to tape the entire joint with one length of tape. If the paper tape wrinkles or bunches up as you embed it with the taping knife, it's probably because you applied the initial layer of compound too thickly or you didn't pull the tape tightly enough when you put it into place. If you have to use two pieces of tape, say, on a joint over 20 ft. long, work from the corner toward the center, where the two pieces overlap.

A butted end joint, such as this one above a doorway, should be reinforced with paper tape to reduce the risk of cracking. Embed the tape in a layer of joint compound, and then smooth out the joint with a taping knife.

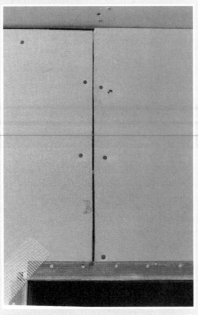

The butted joint should be positioned a few inches in from the edge of the doorway.

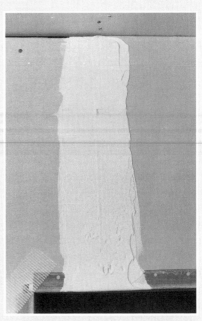

Cover the joint with a layer of joint compound about one trowel width wide.

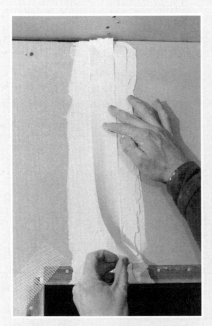

Position the paper tape over the center of the joint, applying light pressure only.

Pull a taping knife along the paper tape, applying enough pressure to push joint compound out from under the tape.

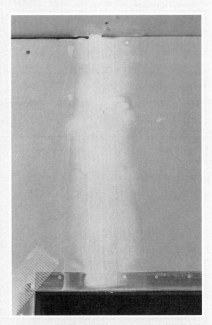

When the first coat is smoothed out, the tape should be embedded in the joint compound and the edges should be feathered out.

Inside corners

Once all the flat seams have been first-coated in the area you're working on, you can move onto the inside corners. Inside corners are a little more difficult to tape than flat seams because it's tricky to get one side of the corner smooth without roughing up the other side. Inside corners should always be taped with paper tape; mesh tape doesn't hold a crease well, and it's easy to cut through the mesh with a taping knife (and easy to sand through it).

Begin by using a taping knife to apply a layer of joint compound approximately 4 in. wide and 1/8 in. or less thick to each edge of the corner. Make sure that the entire inside corner is covered with compound, with no dry areas or unfilled gaps between the panels. Now fold the paper tape along the crease and lightly press it into the corner every 12 in. or so, keeping the tape pulled tight as you go. (Using a tape holder speeds up the process of creasing the tape; see p. 35.) Embed the tape into place with the taping knife, working one edge at a time.

If you're taping an inside corner on a wall, work from top to bottom. If you're taping a long inside corner where the wall meets the ceiling, work from the center toward the ends (see the sidebar

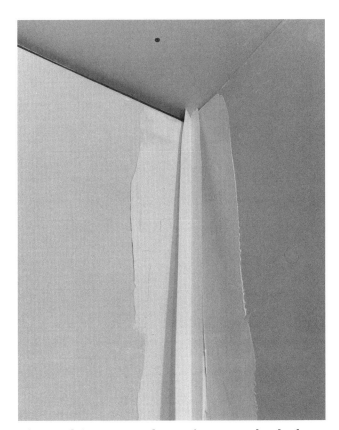

After applying an even layer of compound to both sides of the inside corner, fold the paper tape and position it in the corner.

Press the tape in place with the taping knife one edge at a time. The first coat of compound should be wrinkle-free with feathered-out edges.

below). It will take some practice to embed the tape at each end of the corners without accidentally pulling the tape loose, wrinkling the tape or leaving too much joint compound under the tape. Start with light trowel pressure to embed the tape, and then go over it a few more times with increased pressure to remove the excess joint compound. When you're finished, the first coat on the inside corners should be wrinkle-free and the edges of the com-

TAPING AT CEILING LEVEL

For best results, I prefer to tape the entire length of a seam or inside corner in one pass. That's no problem when you're working on a horizontal wall seam 4 ft. from the floor, but ceilings and the tops of inside or outside corners present more of a challenge.

For ceilings 9 ft. high and under, I find that a pair of adjustable stilts allows me the greatest maneuverability for taping joints and fasteners. If stilts are not practical for you (or if you're not allowed to use them for drywalling where you live), you can set up a plank long enough to work the length of a seam at an appropriate height. For ceilings over 9 ft. high, you'll have to set up some kind of scaffolding, as discussed on pp. 26-27.

In most rooms, all you need to do to reach the top of an inside or outside corner is to step onto an overturned, empty joint-compound pail. I find it easiest to work from the top down.

Working on stilts allows you to tape seams (and fastener heads) in one pass without the need for staging.

Setting a plank on two joint-compound pails below the seam is a simple way to reach the ceiling.

The top of most inside corners can be reached by standing on an empty joint-compound pail.

pound should be feathered out. Some tapers apply a thin coat of joint compound over the tape at this point, but there's no real benefit to this practice; I wait until the corner is dry before applying a second coat.

You can buy special right-angle corner trowels for taping inside corners. A corner trowel has two edges that form an angle slightly greater than 90°, allowing you to work on both sides of the corner simultaneously. I know some contractors

FILLING LARGE GAPS

Drywall isn't always hung perfectly. A problem you sometimes run into when taping inside corners, especially in older homes, is that there's a large gap between panels in the corner. The gap is typically caused by out-of-square or off-level walls or ceilings, or by errors made during measuring.

Sometimes the gap can simply be filled with compound, but if it's wider than ½ in. or so, the compound will fall out. The best remedy for this problem

is to put a layer or two of self-adhesive mesh tape into the corner first. When you apply the joint compound, the mesh will hold it in place. The paper tape can then be positioned in the corner in the normal way.

Allow a little extra time for the corner to dry before applying the next coat of compound because the extra-thick layer of joint compound can crack if second-coated too soon.

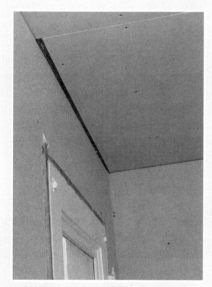

Large gaps at inside corners must be filled with compound before the paper tape is applied.

Affix a layer or two of self-adhesive mesh tape in the corner to provide a surface for the joint compound to cling to.

Apply joint compound to each side of the corner, being careful not to cut through the mesh tape with the edge of the taping knife. Then embed the paper tape.

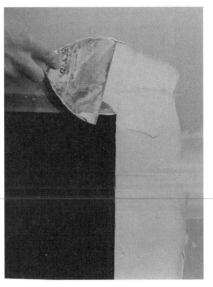

Where two metal corner beads butt together and there is a gap in the drywall, reinforce the area with mesh tape before applying the joint compound.

Cover the corner bead with joint compound the width of the taping knife.

Smooth out the joint compound with a beveled trowel, feathering the edges and leaving the outer edge of the corner bead exposed. Blend the corner in with any seams as you tape.

who use corner trowels all the time, but I've never had much luck with them. I find that taping knives work much better for feathering out the edges.

Outside corners

Right-angle outside corners are a lot easier to tape than inside corners. The corners should have been covered with metal corner bead during the hanging stage (see pp. 58-59), and the corner bead can be first-coated as you work through the room taping the other seams. Just blend in the areas where seams or corners intersect the corner bead.

Cover the metal corner bead with joint compound using a 5-in. or 6-in. taping knife, and then press the compound into place with the edge of a beveled trowel (see the photos above). Using the raised outside edge of the corner bead as a screed, pull the trowel along the corner so that you cover all the metal except

the very outside edge. The inside edge of the joint compound should be feathered out lower than the outside edge of the corner bead.

There is no need to put any tape on the corner bead because it is nailed firmly in place and there are usually no seams or gaps along the corner-bead edge (if there are gaps, use joint tape). If a doorway is wrapped with metal corner bead, you may need to use some fiberglass-mesh tape at the corners to reinforce the area where two pieces of corner bead come together (see the photo at left above).

On corners where you cannot use regular metal corner bead (such as odd-degree corners, corners that are damaged or corners that have inadequate framing for nailing), use flexible metal corner tape, a paper tape that has thin strips of metal attached to either side of the center crease (see pp. 30-31). Cover both sides of the corner with joint compound, being careful not to leave any dry areas or unfilled gaps. (For a strong, durable corner, I recommend you use a setting-type compound for this application.) Cut the corner tape to length with tin snips and fold lightly at the crease.

Press the tape firmly into the joint compound (metal side facing in), and then pull a taping knife along each edge to remove excess compound and embed the tape. Try to keep the very outside edge of the tape tilted out a little so that the edge will act as a screed for the trowel when you're applying the second and third coat of joint compound (essentially, you're trying to mimic the raised outside edge of a metal corner bead). You can tilt the corner tape out with your fingers or with the edge of a trowel.

Embed flexible metal corner tape in a layer of compound with the metal side facing in.

Try to keep the outside edge of the corner tape higher than the panel surface as you smooth out both sides of the corner.

SUMMARY OF FIRST COAT

• Fill any large gaps or holes with joint compound and allow to dry before starting the first coat.

• Apply a thin coat of compound on all screw and nail heads.

• On tapered edge seams, use mesh tape with taping compound or setting-type compounds. Paper tape can be used with taping, setting or all-purpose joint compounds.

• Use paper tape on butted end seams for added strength.

• Use precreased paper tape on all inside corners.

• Keep wrinkles out of paper tape by leaving a smooth, even layer of compound under the tape.

• Don't cover paper tape with joint compound when applying the first coat (it's not wrong, but it's not necessary).

• Don't apply joint compound too thickly.

• Feather out the edges of the compound.

• Blend in compound on outside corners with taped seams as you tape an area.

• Keep the outside edge of metal corner bead as clean as possible.

• Allow the joint compound time to dry thoroughly before applying the second coat.

SECOND COAT

The second coat of joint compound, also known as the filler coat, is the coat during which the largest amount of joint compound is applied. The corner tape is covered and feathered out wider, and the seams are filled and widened. During the second coat, it's important to smooth areas out and blend them together as necessary, but keep in mind that there's still one more coat of compound to apply so everything doesn't have to be perfect. An all-purpose, taping or setting-type compound can be used for the second coat.

Before I begin taping, I usually check over the surface and knock off any noticeable ridges or chunks of hardened compound with the edge of the taping knife. Start the second coat by applying a thin layer of compound to the screw and nail heads, using the same tools and techniques used for the first coat.

Inside corners

After taping the fasteners, I second-coat the inside corners, using a 6-in. taping knife to apply a thin layer of compound to both sides of the corner (see the photos on the facing page). Once the compound is applied, pull the taping knife lightly along the inside edge on one side of the corner, keeping the blade almost flat against the wall. Smooth one side, and then the other, being careful not to rough up the first side too much. Next, hold the knife out from the corner a few inches and feather the outside edge as you remove the excess joint compound. Do this on both sides of the corner. You'll probably have to go over each edge several times to get both edges looking satisfactory. Again, this is not the final coat, so it isn't necessary to get the corner perfect. And it's okay if the paper shows through slightly in spots as long as the taped surface is smooth.

Apply a thin layer of joint compound to each side of the inside corner using a 6-in. taping knife.

Pull the knife along the inside edges of the corner, smoothing the compound and being careful not to mark up the other side of the corner too much.

Hold the knife away from the corner a couple of inches and feather the outside edges as you remove the excess joint compound.

Working both edges together takes some practice, and the taping knife has to be held at just the right angle to avoid taking too much compound off— or leaving too much on. Holding the knife almost flat against the wall and turned out slightly will prevent too much compound from being removed and will also help prevent the knife from marking up the other side of the corner. A steady hand (and a light touch) is also helpful. If the third coat is applied in a similar fashion, very little sanding will be required.

Another way to tape inside corners is to tape one side at a time, allowing it to dry before taping the other side. Each side must be carefully smoothed and feathered out. With this method, one side is taped as the job is second-coated and the other side is taped during the third coat. In other words, the completed corner ends up with only two coats of compound on each side, which means you need to apply the compound a little thicker. And because it's difficult

FIRE-TAPING

Garages, utility rooms and furnace rooms are often hung with fire-resistant drywall. In these non-living areas of the house there's clearly no need to do three coats of taping, but you do have to apply one coat of joint tape and compound to achieve the desired fire rating. This single coat is commonly referred to as fire-taping.

Apply tape and a rough coat of compound to all seams and inside corners in the normal way; you don't have to tape the fastener heads. Outside corners require metal corner bead, which can be attached after you've finished taping but doesn't have to be taped. All gaps wider than $1/16$ in. around pipes, overhead door brackets and other protrusions should also be taped.

to get two coats as smooth as three, a little extra sanding and light touching up with joint compound may be necessary when sanding later.

Tapered edge seams

The second coat of joint compound on seams is usually applied after the inside corners are second-coated, using a 6-in. taping knife and 4-in. by 14-in. beveled trowel. Apply the joint compound with the taping knife about two widths wide, with the seam in the center. The joint compound should be about $3/16$ in. thick and fairly evenly spread. Whenever possible, apply the compound to the entire length of the seam before you start smoothing it. Now use the beveled trowel to smooth out the compound. Keep the trowel almost flat and apply pressure to the outside edges of the seam one edge at a time, feathering out the edges as you pull the trowel along. Some compound will be removed as the edges are feathered out.

Next, center the trowel and glide it along the joint, applying constant even pressure to both edges of the seam. Hold the trowel almost flat against the seam with the back edge doing the work. If all goes well, the edges of the

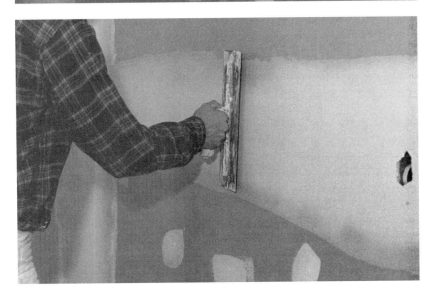

Apply the joint compound evenly, about two knives wide along the seam. On this seam, the opening for the electrical outlet box was patched, making it necessary to go wider in order to blend the patch in with the seam (top). Use a beveled trowel to smooth out the compound, working one edge at a time (center). Finish the seam by gliding the trowel along the center as you apply even pressure to both edges (bottom).

After the second coat has dried, check for potential problem seams with a straightedge or the edge of a long trowel. Hold the straightedge on the center of the seam and check the gap on either side. If it's greater than 1/16 in., you'll need to feather out the compound farther on either side to conceal the seam.

Start at the center and apply joint compound two 6-in. taping knives wide on either side. Build up each side with joint compound, but not the center, and feather out the edges with a beveled trowel.

Check for crowned seams with a straightedge after the second coat has dried.

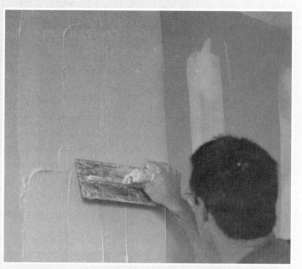

To conceal a crowned seam, apply an extra-wide coat of taping compound. Build up the compound on either side, but leave only a thin layer of compound in the center.

seam will remain feathered and the center will be smoothed to an inconspicuous crown. Repeat this method until most of the air bubbles in the joint compound are smoothed out. The finished second-coat seam should be about 12 in. wide, and the tape should not be visible. Remember, try not to remove too much joint compound. If you find that you're pulling too much off, you're probably holding the trowel at too steep an angle. Apply more compound to the seam and try again, with the trowel held flatter to the surface.

Butted end seams

Because the butted ends of drywall panels are not recessed like the tapered edges, you need to apply a wider band of joint compound to conceal a butted end seam. I usually run my hand across the joint or hold a straightedge to it to determine how wide I need to spread the joint compound to conceal the seam—applying the compound three 6-in. taping knife widths wide usually does the job. The center is the high area, so you need to cover the tape lightly and build up the joint compound along the sides of the tape. Feather out the edges and then smooth the center.

Apply a second coat of joint compound about 12 in. wide to each side of an outside corner.

Use the raised outer edge of the metal corner bead as a screed as you smooth out the sides and feather the edges.

Wherever taped areas intersect they have to be blended together. Here, the author is using a 12-in. straight-handled trowel to blend a seam with an outside corner.

Outside corners

Outside metal corners are easy to second-coat, because the raised outer edge of the corner bead acts as a screed when smoothing out the compound. Apply the joint compound approximately 12 in. wide (the width of two 6-in. taping knives). Switch to a beveled trowel and apply pressure on the outside edge of the joint compound and the edge of the corner bead, holding the trowel almost flat against the compound. When you've finished the second coat, the outer metal edge should still be visible, the center should be smooth and the edges of the compound should be feathered out onto the surface of the panel.

If a seam or an inside corner intersects the outside corner, both areas can be taped at the same time. Blend the areas together, filling and smoothing as necessary using the 6-in. taping knife or a 12-in. straight-handled trowel. You need a very light touch at the intersection—just skim the surface with the edge of the trowel to avoid marking up the other seam (see the bottom photo on the facing page). Blending the two seams together when they are both wet can be tricky, so an alternative is to apply the second coat on the corner and allow it to dry before second-coating the intersecting seam.

THIRD COAT

If you've been careful with the first and second coats, the third coat should be little more than a light skimming over the seams and fasteners, feathering them out a little wider. Very little compound is applied to the surface during this coat.

Light sanding

Because this is the final coat, it's a good idea to do some light sanding before you begin. Sand all the joints and corners using a pole sander with 100-grit or 120-grit sandpaper or sanding screen (see pp. 38-39). Using light pressure, sand up and down each corner and over every seam to remove small ridges, bumps, unfeathered edges, small chunks and trowel marks. Be careful not to sand down to the paper or mesh tape. When sanding outside corners, sand any dry compound off the outside edge of the corner bead. The aim is not to sand out every last defect, but just to make it easier to get the finish coat of joint compound as smooth as possible. Don't take too much time sanding—the average 12-ft. by 12-ft. room should take only about five minutes to go over lightly.

General guidelines

I recommend using a topping or an all-purpose drying-type compound for all third-coat applications. These compounds are easy to apply, can be thinned with water and are easy to sand smooth. Taping compound or setting-type compounds would dry out too quickly on such a thin coat and would also be harder to sand.

Start the third coat by applying a thin layer of compound to the fasteners, and then move on to the seams and outside corners. Wherever these taped areas intersect, smooth and blend them together, working both seams at the same time. Apply the finish coat to the inside corners after the intersecting joints are finished. When applying the third coat, keep the following points in mind:

• The finish coat should be just a little wider than the second coat (see the photo at right).

• All seams should be kept smooth and edges should be kept feathered.

• All scratches and dents should be filled. There should be only a thin layer of joint compound on the rest of the seam.

• All joints should be smooth, with no trowel marks or air bubbles.

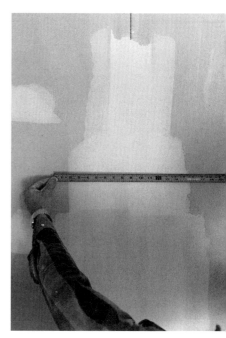

The third coat on a tapered edge seam should be just a little wider than the second coat.

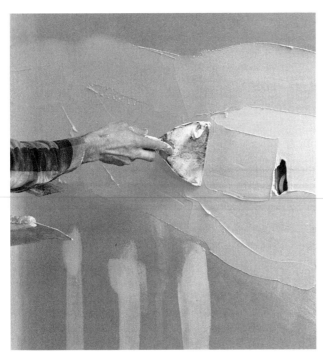

Apply the third coat of joint compound to a seam with a taping knife or wide trowel.

Use a 12-in. taping trowel to remove and smooth the joint compound. Feather the edges first, and then smooth the center.

Seams

There are two ways to apply the finish coat to the seams: with a taping knife (the conventional method) or with a paint roller (the method I prefer).

Taping-knife application Apply the compound with a 6-in. (or wider) taping knife over the entire seam, going slightly wider than the second coat. Next, remove most of the joint compound by pulling a 12-in. trowel firmly along the seam. Feather the edges one last time so that there are no thick or rough spots, and then take off any compound left on the center of the seam. The thin layer of compound left fills in all imperfections, scratches, dents, air bubbles, and so on. The compound will dry out a little as it is worked and can be thinned with water as necessary.

Paint-roller application Thin the joint compound with a little water, and then use a 3/8-in. nap roller to apply the compound, again going just a little wider than the second coat. Then smooth and remove the compound with a 12-in. trowel in the same manner as described for the taping-knife application (see also the sidebar on skim coating on p. 82). I find that rolling works faster than applying the compound by knife, and if you attach a pole to the roller handle it's easy to reach high seams. (Working with a long-handled paint roller is also less stressful on your wrists and arms than applying the compound with a knife or trowel.) One member of the crew can roll the compound on from the floor, while another crew member finishes the seam on stilts.

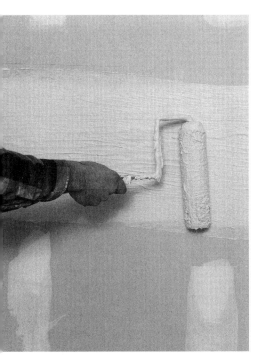

An alternative way to apply the third coat on seams is to use a paint roller.

Inside corners

If you're taping both sides of an inside corner at the same time, follow the same procedure used when second coating (see pp. 74-75). Cover both edges with joint compound just a little wider than the second coat. Remove most of the joint compound, leaving only a thin layer to fill in all imperfections, and feather out the edges. Fill in any voids in the very inside edge left by the trowel or shrinkage of the joint compound.

If you are finishing the inside corners by taping one edge at a time, finish the other edge now (the first edge was second-coated during the last coat; see pp. 75-76). Before taping the second edge, remove any chunks of dried compound that may be in the corners by scraping them off with the taping knife. (Never sand over exposed tape because it may peel off and it's easy to sand through.)

(see pp. 74-75)

ONE-DAY TAPING

The taping method described in this chapter can take anywhere from 48 hours to 72 hours to complete (from initial application of the first coat to complete drying of the third coat). That's fine when you're working through a whole house, but there are times when it's desirable to do all the taping in one day. Fortunately, fast-drying setting-type compounds allow you to do just that.

Setting types of joint compound harden chemically in anywhere from 20 to 30 minutes to 4 to 5 hours, depending on the type of compound used. The compounds with the shortest setting times are ideal for one-day finishing. All three coats can be applied in the same day; and, if the taper is skilled enough, only two coats are necessary because the compound can be put on more heavily since there is very little shrinkage as the compound sets up. Proper temperature, humidity and airflow will help you complete the taping process in one day.

The sequence of steps for one-day taping is as follows:

1. Embed the tape on seams and in corners, and cover any corner bead.

2. Apply the first coat to the fasteners.

3. Apply the second coat to all taped areas as soon as the first coat has set up.

Steps 1 through 3 should be complete by the middle of the working day. Use a compound that sets up in 2 hours or less, or mix the joint compound before it will be needed, which will shorten the setting time after it is applied.

4. After the second coat has hardened, apply the third coat. Use an all-purpose ready-mixed compound or a topping compound for this thin final coat. These compounds are easier to work with—and easier to sand when the third coat is dry.

After the joints and fasteners have been finished with three coats of compound, a thin fourth coat (called a skim coat) can be applied over the entire surface of the drywall panels and joints. Skim coating fills any imperfections in the taped joints and fasteners, smooths the paper surface of the panels, and provides a uniform surface for decorating.

Skim coating is recommended if you're planning to decorate the walls with a high-gloss paint (see pp. 121-122). If you tape only the joints and fasteners, the porosity of the untaped paper surface will be different from that of the taped surface. In addition, the texture will be different—the taped surfaces will be smooth and fine, while the paper surface will be a little rougher. In areas that have been sanded lightly, the paper fibers will be raised. These differences are magnified with the use of gloss paints.

Another time you might consider skim-coating drywall is when remodeling—for example, if you're trying to blend new drywall panels with an existing plaster surface. Skim coating helps minimize the difference in texture between the different surfaces and gives the appearance that the wall is all plaster.

To apply the skim coat, use a long-nap roller ($\frac{3}{8}$ in. is fine) and an all-purpose ready-mixed or topping compound that has been thinned with a little water. Roll a thin coat of compound over the entire surface, and then immediately smooth it with a trowel or a taping knife, working each area until it is free of all imperfections.

To skim-coat a wall, roll on a layer of slightly thinned joint compound over the entire surface.

Applying firm pressure, smooth the compound with a wide trowel or taping knife.

A final check

Once you've applied the final coat and before you start sanding, walk through each room to check that the taping job is satisfactory. Look over the seams and corners, checking for indentations, scratches or any areas where the tape shows through. Touch up any imperfections with a thin application of joint compound before going on to the finish-sanding process (see Chapter 5). If anything requires special attention, such as a crack, a crowned seam or an over-cut outlet box, correct these areas now before you begin sanding.

TAPING PROBLEMS

As is probably obvious if you've read this far, joints between panels can be a potential problem area. Some problems will become apparent while you're taping; other problems you may not notice until after the wall or ceiling has been painted. In this section, I'll describe the most common problems, explain how to correct them and suggest ways to avoid them in the first place.

Photographing

Photographing is a problem that can occur if a wall or ceiling is painted with a gloss paint (high gloss, semi-gloss or even a satin finish). When seen in direct natural light, the seams and strips of taped fasteners may still show even though they were taped and sanded correctly. Photographing is caused by the different porosities and textures of the panel surface and the taped joints.

This condition can be prevented by skim coating the entire surface before painting (see the sidebar on the facing page), or by using a good-quality primer-sealer or a flat latex paint before applying the finish coat of paint (see Chapter 8). If you notice photographing after the drywall has been painted, lightly sand the surface using 150-grit sandpaper and then paint with a good-quality flat latex paint before recoating with the finish paint.

Crowned and concave seams

Crowned seams occur when taping compound is applied too heavily and the center of the seam is left higher than the surface of the panels. When light shines across the seams, they will be quite obvious. If the seams have not been painted, the crowned areas can be sanded down with 120-grit or 150-grit paper. If they have already been painted, it would be difficult to sand the areas (which is why it's important to check for crowned seams during the final check), but the seams can be widened on each side of the crowned area. Feather the joint compound out on either side, being careful not to raise the crowned area any higher. Check the joint with a straight-edge when the compound is dry. If the crown has been corrected, apply a finish coat of compound before sanding.

Concave seams are the exact opposite of crowned seams. These defects, which show as a slight depression along the taped seams when light shines across the joints, are usually the result of not applying the joint compound heavily enough during the second coat. Concave seams can also be caused by oversanding. To correct the problem, reapply the second and third coats of joint compound.

Pitting

Pitting looks like a series of small pits or craters on the taped finish surface (see the photo at left on p. 84). The pits are small air bubbles that were not filled in properly or were exposed when sanding. The air bubbles are the result of the joint compound being overmixed or mixed too thin. Small air bubbles may also appear on the wet joint-compound surface if insufficient pressure is applied when smoothing the joint compound.

If a large number of air bubbles appear as you tape, keep going over the joints with the trowel, applying more pressure until most of the bubbles are gone. If

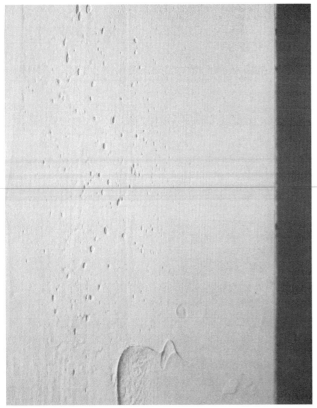

Pitting is caused by small air bubbles in the joint compound.

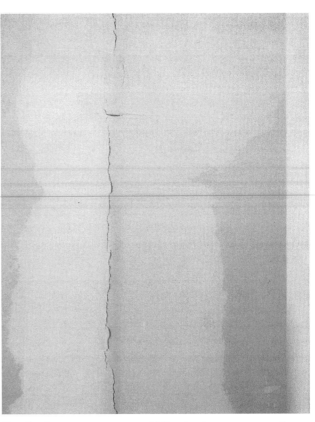

Cracked seams can occur if the taping compound dries too quickly or is applied too thickly.

you don't notice the bubbles until the surface has been painted, apply a thin finish coat over the problem areas. Then sand and prime the retaped areas before repainting.

Cracked and shrinking seams

If seams crack during the taping process, it's usually because the joint compound dried too quickly (as a result of direct high heat or sunlight). As long as the tape and the joint compound are still solid, you can retape the cracked area. Make sure that the seam is thoroughly dry before you work on it, and use enough pressure to force the compound into the crack. If the tape is cracked or the compound is loose, you'll have to remove the affected areas. Cracked seams can be avoided by lowering the heat to increase the drying time. If the

outside temperature is warm (above 80°F), close the windows so the airflow will not dry out the compound too fast.

Although it may sound contradictory, cracked seams may also be the result of the joint compound drying too slowly. If a second coat is applied over a first coat that is still damp, the compound may shrink excessively. As the compound dries, cracks will form where the joint compound is the thickest. Any loose areas should be removed and filled with joint compound before retaping and finishing. To avoid this problem, make sure the building is heated more efficiently (to at least 60°F to 65°F) and keep the humidity low (by opening or closing windows, running fans or raising the temperature). In addition, be sure the previous coat of joint compound is thoroughly dry before applying the next coat.

Shrinking that appears along the center of taped seams after sanding is a related problem that is also caused by taping over a coat of joint compound that has not thoroughly dried. Remember that joint compound usually dries on the outside edges first, so a seam that appears dry may still be wet underneath. To correct the slightly recessed area caused by shrinkage, apply a layer of compound to fill the area and then sand lightly.

Bubbled tape

Bubbled or loose paper tape results when the bond between the tape and joint compound is poor. If the tape is not properly embedded in the compound, it can come loose and raise a bubble. The bubble may be a round spot only ½ in. in diameter or it may run the entire length of a seam. Small bubbles can be cut out with a utility knife and retaped. For larger loose areas, the whole section of tape should be removed and new tape embedded, followed by a second and third coat of joint compound. The problem of bubbled or loose tape can be avoided by making sure that you apply a thick enough layer of joint compound before you embed the tape and apply enough pressure with the taping knife to embed the tape properly.

Popped nails and screws

Nail and screw pops don't usually show up until several months or years after the original taping job, but they do occasionally become apparent before you paint. Quite a bit of pressure is applied against the panel when using a pole sander to sand the fasteners, and if a screw or nail has not pulled the panel tight against the framing, the pressure of the pole sander can push the panel tight and cause the fasteners to "pop," raising a pronounced bump on the surface or exposing the fastener head.

If fastener pops appear before you paint, refasten the panel while applying hand pressure next to the fastener to ensure that the panel is tight against the framing. The loose screws or nails should be reset or removed. Retape the fasteners with three thin coats of joint compound. If the drywall surface is damaged around the fastener, place a piece of mesh tape over the damaged area first. (For more on repairing fastener pops, see Chapter 7.)

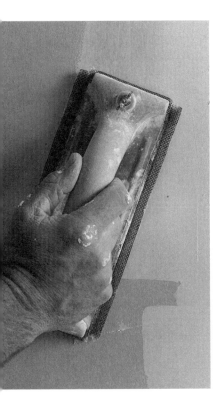

5
SANDING

If taping is my favorite part of a drywalling job, I'd have to say that sanding is my least favorite. The dust makes the job unpleasant, and it is tedious (and fairly difficult) work. Sanding is the final step in the drywalling process—and, in my opinion, also the most important. It's your last chance before painting to turn a so-so taping job into a quality finished job.

Some tapers claim to be so skillful at taping that they don't need to sand at all. With my experience as a drywall contractor, however, I believe that a beautiful finished job requires at least some sanding after the final coat. (Depending on your taping ability, you may need to sand between coats as well, as discussed on p. 79.) I have painted ceilings prior to texturing that I have not sanded at all. In most light these ceilings look just fine, but most customers I've worked with aren't satisfied with a finished job that looks good in most light. They want a job that looks good all the time and in any light.

Sanding is a dusty and time-consuming process. It takes me almost as much time to sand as it does to apply one coat of joint compound (just under an hour for a typical 12-ft. by 12-ft. room). You have to sand all the taped seams, corners and fastener heads, and you end up going over a large percentage of the drywall surface area. But if you take your time and have the right attitude (just keep in mind that once you're done you can start painting), the results are rewarding.

GETTING READY TO SAND

Because sanding joint compound creates so much dust, you'll need to wear a dust mask, which should be approved for protection against non-toxic dust and mist. In order for the mask to work to your benefit, it should fit snugly. When you breathe through the mask, air should not enter around the edges. (If air does get in, you'll notice white dust on your face around the edges of the mask when you take the mask off after sanding.) Change the filter or mask when breathing becomes difficult. It's also a good idea to wear a hat and safety goggles for protection against the fine dust, especially when you're sanding overhead.

You'll not only need to protect yourself while sanding, but also the room you're working in (unless, of course, you're drywalling in new construction). On a remodeling job, all furnishings should have been removed or covered with drop cloths and plastic before drywalling began. The fine dust generated during sanding can infiltrate the tiniest of cracks, so make sure to seal under all doors (including kitchen cabinets) to keep the dust from spreading. Seal the edges of the plastic with masking tape.

THE SANDING PROCESS

You could conceivably use power sanders to sand joint compound, but I do all my sanding with hand-powered tools (primarily a pole sander). An electric sander, such as a belt or disc sander, will cut through joint compound fast, but it is very hard to control and will almost certainly destroy the joint and dig up the drywall panels. Sanding is a two-step process. First, I use the pole sander to remove excess joint compound, such as marks left by taping tools, crowned areas where too much compound was applied and intersecting joints that need to be blended. Then I do a final sanding with one or more hand tools.

Pole sanding

A pole sander fitted with a 120-grit sanding screen does an excellent job of smoothing the edges of the seams. If you're sanding a nice, smooth taping job, you can use the finer 150-grit sandpaper or sanding screen. It doesn't cut through the joint compound as quickly as 120 grit and is gentler on the drywall paper surface (whatever grit you're using, be careful not to oversand the face paper). The 150 grit works well with lightweight joint compounds or with topping compounds; these compounds are slightly softer than all-purpose compound and scratch more easily with the coarser grits of sanding paper.

Push the pole sander along the seams and outside corners in the direction of the seam or corner, using a gentle, even pressure. Keep the edges smooth, and sand down any high spots or chunks of joint compound on the seams. Run the pole sander over the entire taped area. Be especially careful when sanding inside corners, because there is only a thin layer of joint compound covering the paper

Dust masks should be comfortable, form a good seal around the edges and be approved for protection against non-toxic dust and mist. The top mask shown here has a replaceable filter.

Use a pole sander to blend the edges of seams and sand down any high spots. The 4-ft. handle allows plenty of leverage and keeps you at least an arm's length away from the dusty sanded surface.

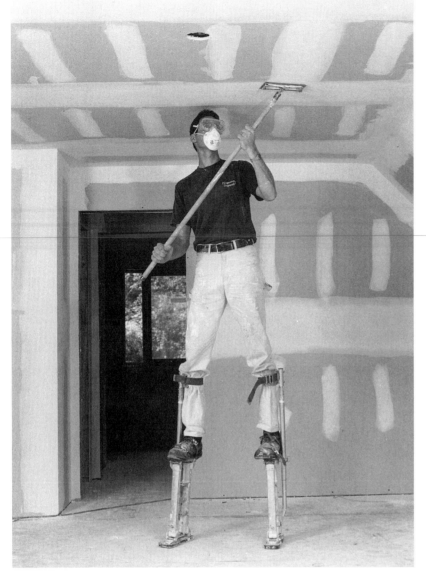

Working on stilts can make the job of sanding ceilings easier. Wear goggles or glasses to protect your eyes from the dust.

tape. Sand to blend the edges in smoothly, and go along the inside edge only lightly with the pole sander. The inside edge will be finish-sanded later with a hand sander, dry sanding sponge or folded piece of sanding material.

Sand the screw or nail heads lightly in the direction of the strip of joint compound. Check the edges to make sure they are smooth. When sanding screws, you'll be putting pressure on the drywall around the screw head. If the screw has not properly pulled the drywall panel tight against the framing, it may pop loose under the pressure. The joint compound may come off the screw head, or you may see the drywall move in and out around the screw. To correct the problem, use a Phillips screwdriver and turn the screw until it is tight again. If it goes too deep into the drywall or will not tighten up, place another screw about 1½ in. away and then retape the area with three coats of joint compound.

Even though you can reach most ceilings with a pole sander from the floor, I prefer to work on stilts. Using the stilts gets me close to the surface of the ceiling, where I can see the area that I am sanding a lot better. Also, most of the dust settles away from my face instead

OVERSANDING

If you do too much sanding (a common problem with beginners) and expose the joint tape or damage the drywall face paper, you may have to apply the third coat again. In more serious cases, you may even need to reapply the second and third coats.

If the sandpaper you're using is too coarse, you may put scratches in the compound or drywall paper. In such cases, try sanding lightly with a finer sandpaper or sanding screen, such as 200 grit. If the scratches still show, apply a thin finishing coat of compound and resand lightly when dry.

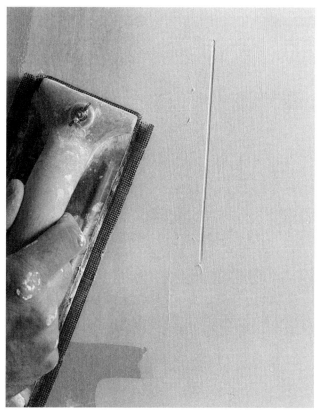

Some scratches in the joint compound are too deep to sand out without oversanding the surrounding area.

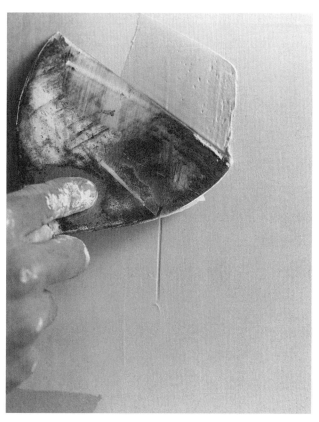

Instead of sanding, fill the area with a thin layer of joint compound and then resand after the compound has dried.

of into it. (Wear safety goggles or glasses to help keep the dust out of your eyes.)

Don't try to get out every last defect with the pole sander—you may end up sanding out the scratch or dent, but in the process oversand the entire area. Some defects may need to be filled with joint compound and then sanded again later, so it's a good idea to keep a trowel with a small amount of joint compound handy. Fill in the defects as you go along, so they will not be overlooked (see the photos above).

While sanding, if you notice a seam that is still indented or slightly crowned, you may need to apply a third coat or, in a worse case, a second and third coat of joint compound. A good way to check to see if a seam is crowned too much is to hold the edge of a wide trowel across it (see the drawing on p. 90). If the trowel rocks more than $1/16$ in. on either side of the center of the seam, you may want to widen the seam by feathering the joint compound out on each side, being careful not to add any to the crowned center. If the trowel indicates a recess of over $1/16$ in., fill in the seam with joint compound as necessary and then reapply the third coat.

CHECKING FOR PROBLEM SEAMS

Hold the straight edge of a wide trowel across the seam to check for crowns (or recesses).

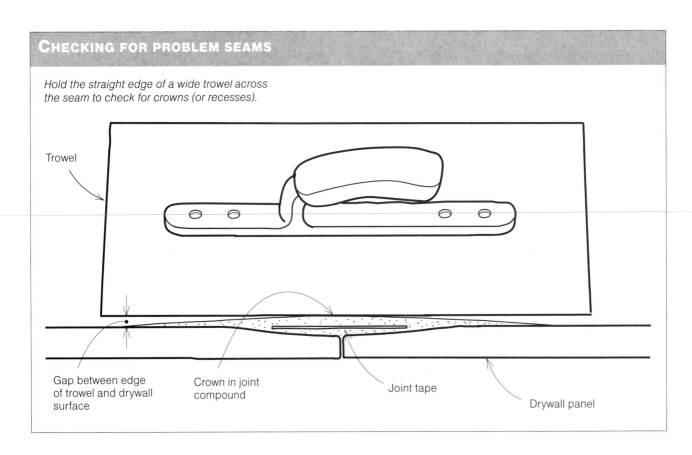

Trowel

Gap between edge
of trowel and drywall
surface

Crown in joint
compound

Joint tape

Drywall panel

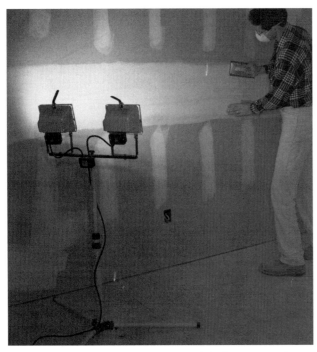

Shining a bright light along a wall helps you pick out problem areas during the final sanding.

As you go over the compound with a hand sander, look and feel for any defects that need to be sanded out.

Finish sanding

After all the taped surfaces have been sanded with a pole sander, I switch to a hand sander for the finish sanding. I'll also use a dry sanding sponge and a folded piece of sandpaper or screen for the finish work. Before you get started, make sure you have adequate lighting. A bright light shining along a wall or a ceiling will help highlight defects or problems you might not see with poor lighting or with natural lighting alone (see the photo at left on the facing page).

Use a hand sander, fitted with 150-grit or finer sanding paper or a sanding screen, to go over all seams, corners and fasteners. Look and feel for any defects. Lightly sand out these areas and any edges that are not feathered out properly. Once again, remember not to oversand. If a defect is deep or if you sand through to the tape, repair the area with a thin coat of joint compound. Mark these areas with a pencil (a pen or marker will bleed through most paints) and go back later and resand if necessary.

Use a dry sanding sponge, a folded piece of sandpaper or sanding screen to sand out small defects. I prefer to use the fine-grit dry sanding sponge to smooth both edges of an inside corner (at the same time) and to touch up the compound around an electrical outlet. You have to be careful around electrical boxes because the face paper of the dry-wall tears easily where it has been cut. I use a folded piece of sandpaper or sanding screen to get into spots where the other sanders can't reach without damaging the area around the defect.

A fine-grit dry sanding sponge can be used to sand both inside edges of a corner at the same time.

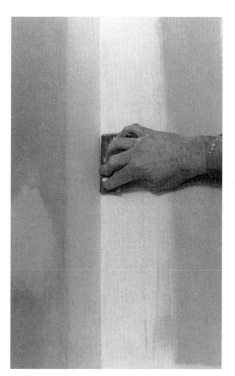

A folded piece of sanding screen or sandpaper helps keep inside corners clean and straight.

DUST-FREE SANDERS

For those sanding jobs where you really have to keep the dust down, you might want to try a dust-free sander. This tool, which is relatively new to the market, is a pole or hand sander with an attachment that fits on a wet/dry vacuum. It is used in exactly the same way as a regular pole or hand sander—the only difference is that most of the dust ends up in the vacuum cleaner, not on the floor. The model I use is designed as a pole sander, but you can remove the handle, reattach the hose and use it as a hand sander.

A dust-free pole sander attaches to a wet/dry vacuum, which sucks up most of the dust as the sanding is being done.

Make sure to remove and sand hardened chunks of joint compound from taped seams and corners wherever they butt up against a floor, a window or a door. These areas have to be smooth so that the trim or casing will lie flat against the wall. Use the corner of a taping knife to clean any hardened compound out of electrical boxes (be careful not to cut the wire!).

General cleanup

After you've finished sanding, the cleanup can begin. I use a wet/dry vacuum cleaner for this task, making sure to vacuum (or brush) out all the electrical boxes, around the window and door frames and along the edge of the floor against the walls. It's a real pain to have

your brush or roller pick up dust or chunks of compound while painting, so do a thorough job.

In new construction, I recommend scraping hardened chunks of compound off the floor and then sweeping up the mess. A vacuum or a wet mop will pick up most of the remaining dust. If you've used drop cloths and plastic, carefully roll them up and shake them off outside. You'll probably still need to vacuum the floor or carpet, especially around the edges.

WET SANDING

Occasionally you may be working on a job where no dust at all is acceptable—for example, in an office building that contains sensitive computer equipment or a home where a family member is allergic to dust particles. Even with careful covering and sealing of the work area, the fine dust that is created when sanding is still going to get into unwanted areas.

In cases like these, there is an alternative sanding method: wet sanding, or sponging. Since joint compound is water-soluble, the edges of taped areas and small defects can be blended in with a wet sponge. When only a small touchup is required, an all-purpose household sponge or even a smooth, soft cloth will work effectively. For a larger wet-sanding job, use a high-density polyurethane sponge made specially for this purpose. The drywall sponge has small cells, which help it to retain water without excessive dripping.

Wait until the finished coat of joint compound is dry before you start wet sanding. If you don't, any joint compound placed in the scratches or low areas may be pulled out by the sponge, and these defects will still show after drying. To wet sand, dip the sponge in clean, cool water that contains no soap or additives. Do not wring all the water

	Advantages	Disadvantages
Dry sanding	• cuts down high spots easily • most crowns and edges can be sanded out • faster than wet sanding • pole sander can be used to reach high areas without a bench or scaffold • excellent results after three coats of joint compound	• very dusty • easy to oversand • need to wear dust mask
Wet sanding	• not dusty • fewer tools required • easier cleanup of work areas • no need to wear dust mask	• requires better taping job • will not correct large defects • just blends the area • slower than dry sanding

out of the sponge, just enough to eliminate dripping. Clean the sponge frequently during use. As when dry-sanding, rub the sponge in the direction of the seam or corner. Avoid rubbing across a seam or into a corner too much, because this may cause rippling in the finish. Use as few strokes as possible, and be careful not to soak the joint compound. If the sponge is too wet, water may run down the walls, and streaks will be visible when it dries. In addition, avoid excessive wetting of the drywall paper surface, since it can rip easily when wet.

While wet sanding is effective for blending the edges of taped seams and small defects, it doesn't work so well on ridges or larger chunks. The sponge just blends or rounds an area over, in contrast to sandpaper, which cuts an area down. If you plan to wet sand, make sure to do an extra good job of taping. After the third coat of joint compound is dry, examine the surface carefully using a bright light to help highlight any problem areas. Apply a thin coat of joint compound to these areas and allow to dry before wet sanding.

When wet sanding, use a wet (but not dripping) sponge to smooth out taped areas, rubbing the sponge back and forth in the direction of the seam, corner or fastener strip.

6

SPECIAL
INSTALLATIONS

If all walls were straight and square with no butted seams and all corners were 90°, drywalling would be a rather mechanical and predictable job. But, as anyone who is trying their hand at drywalling will soon find out, problem areas or unusual seams or corners will sooner or later present themselves. These situations might be as simple as having to install extra fasteners to meet fire-code regulations or as complicated as having to bend drywall panels around a curved wall with a very tight radius.

In this chapter, I'll explain how to tape rounded corners, archways and curved walls, how to handle butt joints (if they're unavoidable) and drywall that must be hung next to a tub or shower, and how to install multiple layers of drywall. In addition, I'll explain how to use resilient steel channel and how to work with cement board. Most of these special installations are really not much harder than hanging drywall on a straight wall or ceiling, as long as you understand how to approach them and use the right techniques.

ROUNDED CORNERS

When a sloped ceiling meets a flat ceiling or a wall, the corner formed is usually much greater than 90°. While it's relatively easy to keep a 90° corner straight when hanging and taping drywall, it's much harder to get a good, even finish on corners that are greater than 90°, especially if the corner is long. To avoid crooked corners, I finish any corner that is 120° or wider (and longer than 4 ft.) by "rounding" it slightly (see the drawing on the facing page). Rounding the corner makes it appear straighter because there is no obvious interior angle.

As with regular inside corners, rounded corners can be finished with three coats of joint compound. I recommend using fiberglass-mesh tape combined with a setting-type joint compound for the first coat. First, cover the corner with the mesh tape, as shown in the photo at left on the facing page. If there are large gaps between panels or damaged areas, apply an additional piece of mesh tape to cover these areas. Next, use a 6-in. taping knife to apply a thin coat of joint compound to each side of the corner, as shown in the photo at right on the facing page. At this stage, it's not necessary to cover the tape completely—a layer about ⅛ in. thick and 4 in. or 5 in. wide is sufficient.

Once you've applied the compound, pull the taping knife across the corner at a 90° angle (see the photo at left on p. 96). After you've gone across the corner in one direction, there will still be gaps and rough edges in the compound;

When taping an inside corner that forms an angle greater than 120°, use mesh tape to cover the joint.

Use a 6-in. taping knife to apply a thin layer of joint compound about 4 in. or 5 in. wide to each side of the joint.

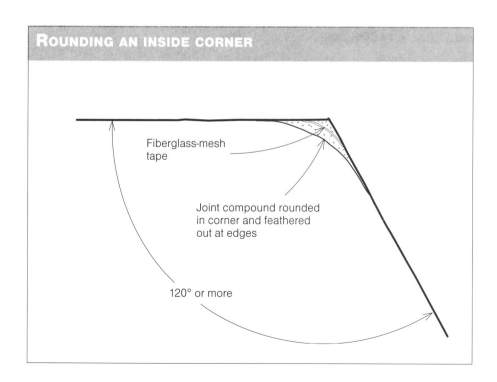

ROUNDING AN INSIDE CORNER

Fiberglass-mesh tape

Joint compound rounded in corner and feathered out at edges

120° or more

Pull the trowel gently across the corner in one direction for the length of the joint; then pull the trowel back across the corner in the opposite direction. The center of the joint should be filled and slightly rounded, while the edges are feathered out.

Use a 12-in. trowel to round over the corners after applying the second coat.

to correct these areas, pull the knife across the corner in the opposite direction. Take your time, and don't apply too much pressure (very little joint compound should be removed if you're doing it right). As you pull the knife gently across the corner, each edge of the compound should be feathered out and the center should be slightly rounded. The tape should now be completely covered, and there should be no large gaps or high ridges left by the knife.

For the second coat on a rounded corner, use a setting-type compound, an all-purpose compound or a ready-mixed taping compound. I prefer to use a setting-type compound for this coat because a pretty heavy layer of compound is left in the rounded area of the

corner, which can result in excessive shrinkage if you use a drying type. The shrinkage could cause a deep crack that would require reinforcement with tape to correct. Using a 6-in. knife, apply about the same amount of compound to each side of the corner as you did during the first coat. On this coat, use a 12-in. straight-handled trowel to round the compound (see the photo above). Pull the trowel across the corner in one direction and then in the opposite direction, just as you did for the first coat. Once again, very little compound should be removed as the corner is rounded and the edges are feathered.

Before applying the third coat, lightly sand out any high trowel marks and feather the edges with a pole sander

A paint roller works well for applying the third coat of joint compound to a rounded corner.

Smooth out the joint compound with a 12-in. trowel.

and a 120-grit sanding screen or paper (be careful not to oversand or dig up the center areas). For the third coat of joint compound, use a topping or an all-purpose ready-mixed compound. You can apply the compound with a 6-in. or 12-in. knife, but I find that a roller works best since it easily follows the curve of the rounded corner (see the photo above). Cover the entire taped area with a thin layer of joint compound and widen out each edge. Then use the 12-in. trowel to remove the joint compound, in much the same way that a third coat on a regular seam is finished (see p. 80). All trowel marks and indentations should be filled, and only a thin film of compound should remain on the rest of the corner.

CURVED WALLS

Drywall can be formed to fit almost any curved surface (convex or concave). Depending on the radius of the curve, it can be applied wet or dry.

The first curved surface I ever tried to drywall was a convex wall with a very short radius. (Walls with a short radius—32 in. or less—form a tight curve; walls with a longer radius—32 in. or more—form a gentler curve.) At that time, the only advice I'd been given was to wet a regular ½-in. drywall panel and allow it to sit for awhile before hanging. Given my lack of experience, it's not surprising that I didn't have much luck with this job. I ended up having to cut the dry-

Quarter-inch flexible drywall can be formed to fit convex and concave wall surfaces.

tight curve. If you are planning to attach drywall to a curved surface, here are a few important points to bear in mind:

• To help prevent flat areas between studs, the framing should be closer together on curved walls than on straight walls. Maximum stud spacing is 9 in. on center for most curves; for really short radii, 6 in. on center maximum is recommended (see the chart on p. 8). Don't try to drywall an inside curve that has a radius under 20 in. or an outside curve under 15 in.; these curves are too tight, and the panels will break.

• Use ¼-in. flexible drywall for both inside (concave) and outside (convex) curves. Attach the drywall horizontally and place the screws a maximum of 12 in. on center. Two layers of ¼ in. are usually necessary for strength and to blend in with ½-in. drywall used on straight sections of the wall. Apply one layer at a time, staggering the joints. If possible, avoid end joints butted on the curved surface of the wall.

• If the radius of the curve is 32 in. or more, ¼-in. flexible drywall panels can usually be applied dry. It may be helpful to prebow the panels overnight by standing them on end against a wall or by supporting each end off the floor, allowing the center to bow (see the drawing on p. 50).

• If the radius of the curve is less than 32 in., the drywall will have to be damp-ened in order to conform to the tight curve without breaking. Using a garden sprayer, a sponge or a paint roller (see the top photo on the facing page), apply water to the side that is going to be compressed when formed around the curve (i.e., the back of the panel on con-vex curves). For a ¼-in., 4x8 panel use about 30 oz. of water (35 oz. for a ⅜-in. panel, 45 oz. for a ½-in. panel). Stack the panels with the wet surfaces facing each other and let them sit for at least

wall, which I had wet on both sides, into narrow strips in order to get it to bend around the studs. After the narrow strips dried, I had to tape each seam and then skim-coat the entire surface.

Looking back, I realize what I did wrong. First, the wall was much too tightly curved to bend a ½-in. drywall panel around. Second, I should not have wet both sides of the panel. Third, the studs were spaced too far apart for such a

For walls with a tight curve, dampen one side of the drywall panel before it is attached.

one hour before you attach them. When the panels dry, they will return to their original hardness.

• When attaching drywall on the outside of a curved wall, start at one end of the curve and fasten the panel to the studs as it is formed around the curve (see the photo on the facing page). When dry-walling the inside of a curved wall, start by attaching the panel at the center of the curve and fasten to each stud as the panel is formed out toward the edges (see the photo at right).

• When taping the seams on a curved wall, use either mesh tape or paper tape and apply three coats of joint compound in the usual manner. If the drywall is wet, allow enough time for it to dry thoroughly before taping.

When fastening drywall to the concave side of a wall, begin at the center of the curve and then work out toward the edges.

ARCHWAYS

Drywalling a curved archway is a similar process to drywalling a curved wall. As with curved walls, ¼-in. flexible drywall works best for short-radius archways (on gentler arches you can use regular ¼-in. drywall or even ½ in.). Cut the drywall to the desired width and approximate length. Screw or nail the strip into place starting at the center and working toward the edges, as shown in the photo below. If you're using ¼-in. drywall, you may need two layers to blend in with the sides of the archway and also for added strength.

If you don't want to buy a whole sheet of ¼-in. flexible drywall just to do one archway, then you can use ½-in. regular drywall instead. In this case, score the back paper of the drywall strip at 1-in. intervals (or closer if the curve is tight). As the strip is fastened into place around the arch, the back will separate at the cuts, allowing the drywall to conform to the shape of the curve (see the top photo at left on the facing page).

After the drywall has been attached to all sides of the archway, attach corner bead to the outside edges. Flexible vinyl corner bead works best for this application because it is precut every inch along one side and it bends uniformly around the curve. Start at one end of the archway and nail or screw the corner into place along the wall surface of the archway as necessary in order to keep the corner snug against the wall and the curved surface (see the top photo at right, facing page). If you can't find flexible vinyl corner bead, you can cut a regular metal corner bead with tin snips every inch along one side (see the bottom photo at left, facing page) and attach it in the same manner.

Once the corner bead has been fastened to the archway, attach metal corner bead to the vertical sides (see the bottom photo at right, facing page). Make sure that the surfaces are flush and fitted together evenly where the two corner beads butt together. Tape the corner bead on the archway in the same manner as any corner bead.

To drywall the inside of an archway, cut a strip of ¼-in. flexible drywall to width and fasten into place, working from the center out.

Half-inch drywall will conform to an archway if the back paper is scored at regular intervals across its width.

Attach flexible vinyl corner bead to the outside edges of the archway.

You can use regular metal corner bead on an archway by making cuts along one edge of the bead.

Cover the straight sides of an archway with metal corner bead, taking care to butt the adjoining pieces of corner bead together evenly.

BUTTED SEAMS

Throughout this book, I have stressed the importance of trying to avoid butted seams between the untapered ends of panels wherever possible. If you have to use butted joints, make sure to keep them away from the center of the wall or ceiling and take time to feather out the taped joints carefully. No matter how careful a job you do, however, the joints may still be visible after the room is painted. I'm embarrassed to say that I found this out when I returned to a job to take some photos for this book—what had looked like a perfect job the day I'd finished it had developed slight ridges at the center of the butted joints. The deformation, known in the trade as "ridging," was only visible in certain lighting, but it was enough to bother me.

Ridging

Building materials expand or contract as the temperature and humidity inside a building change. As the building materials move, tension builds up against the drywall panels. The tension is relieved as the panels bend outward, usually at a joint. Over time, the slight ridge becomes more stable and any additional movement will have no effect on the drywall.

Ridging can occur in regular tapered edge seams, but it is much more common in butted end joints. After the ridging has stopped, typically in six months to a year, the joint can be hidden by applying joint compound to either side of the ridge and feathering it out into the panel surface (see the discussion of crowned seams in the sidebar on p. 77). There are, however, a couple of ways to minimize ridging in the first place: by back-blocking with drywall or by back-blocking with plywood.

Back-blocking with drywall Back-blocking is designed to minimize ridging by placing butt joints between framing members (see the top drawing on the facing page). The drywall has to be hung perpendicular to the framing members so that the butt ends can be reinforced with pieces of drywall that are laminated to the back of each panel, behind the joint.

Begin by cutting two strips of drywall 3 in. wide by 4 ft. long and nail them along the edge of the studs or joists that the joint will fall between. Keep the drywall strips set back from the framing surface about ⅛ in. more than the thickness of the drywall. Next cut a piece of drywall 48 in. long and slightly narrower than the width between the framing. Cover this narrow piece of drywall with joint compound, and use a notched trowel to leave beads of compound that are ½ in. high, ⅜ in. wide and spaced ½ in. on center. Toe-nail the piece in place between the studs with the joint compound facing out.

Now hang the drywall, centering the butted seam between the framing, and fasten to the framing in the usual way. Attach the two panels so that the butted joint fits snug, but not tightly. Next place a ¼-in. thick by 1-in. wide strip of wood along the length of the joint to create a recess for taping; hold the strip in place by fastening a temporary drywall brace over the joint, screwing it into place along the framing members on either side of the joint. The next day, remove the brace and the wood strip. The joint will be slightly recessed for easy finishing.

Back-blocking with plywood Back-blocking using drywall and joint compound is a good way to reduce ridging and the finished results are excellent, but it is clearly time-consuming. As an alternative, you can use plywood as a backer, as shown in the bottom drawing on the facing page.

To back-block with plywood, hang the first drywall panel so that the butted seam falls in between two framing members. Now attach a strip of plywood (½ in. thick by about 10 in. wide and

48 in. long) along the back of the butted seam using drywall screws. (Don't use a 2x6 or a wider piece of plywood because it could cause the drywall to sag slightly at the joint.) Hang the abutting piece of drywall, securing it to the framing member and to the plywood in the same manner. The butted seam is now a solid part of the drywall panel, and it is located away from the framing member.

To create a butted seam that is easier to hide, attach a thin piece of wood or cardboard (about 1/8 in. thick) along each edge of the plywood. When the drywall is screwed along the center of the plywood, the thin shims will cause the joint to bow in, which will create a slight recess. This recess will make the joint easier to hide when taping.

BACK-BLOCKING WITH DRYWALL

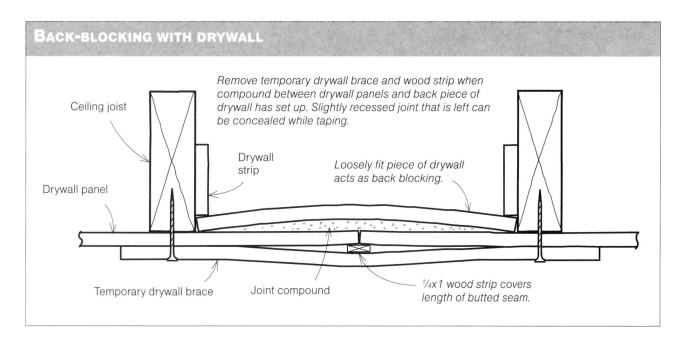

Ceiling joist

Drywall strip

Remove temporary drywall brace and wood strip when compound between drywall panels and back piece of drywall has set up. Slightly recessed joint that is left can be concealed while taping.

Loosely fit piece of drywall acts as back blocking.

Drywall panel

Temporary drywall brace

Joint compound

1/4x1 wood strip covers length of butted seam.

BACK-BLOCKING WITH PLYWOOD

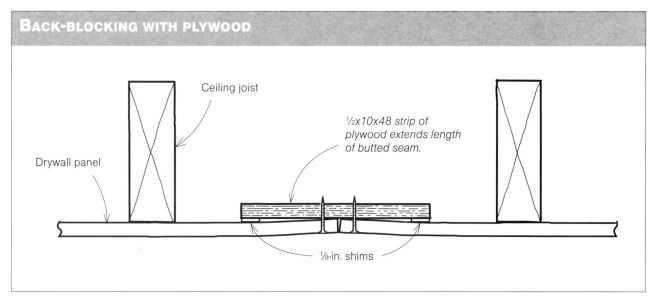

Ceiling joist

1/2x10x48 strip of plywood extends length of butted seam.

Drywall panel

1/8-in. shims

FLAT TAPING

When drywall is butted up against a tub/shower unit, trim work or a wooden beam, it can be very difficult to fit each panel perfectly so that there are no gaps or broken edges. These areas have to be taped for a quality finish.

Start by fitting the drywall as closely as possible to the abutting surface, and then fasten the drywall securely along the edge. To avoid a crack around the edge, also make sure that the abutting surface is securely fastened. After proper attachment, fill in any gaps wider than ¼ in. with joint compound and allow time for them to dry. Then apply fiberglass-mesh tape around the edges being fitted and apply a layer of joint compound approximately 4 in. wide with a taping knife. Smooth the layer of compound out and feather the outside edges, leaving enough compound over the tape to conceal it. Let the compound dry and apply a second and then a third coat using the same techniques used to tape one edge of an inside corner (see pp. 74-75).

Before taping around a raised surface such as a tub/shower unit, fill in any large gaps with joint compound and allow to dry (top left). Apply fiberglass-mesh tape tight against the tub/shower unit, and cover with a thin layer of joint compound (above). Apply a second and third coat of compound, feathering the edges and keeping the tub/shower unit as clean of compound as possible (bottom left).

During each application of joint compound try to keep the compound off the adjoining surface, especially if the surface is natural wood trim or a fiberglass shower unit. It's easy to scratch these surfaces with taping knives (or with sandpaper when sanding). Wash any joint compound off the surface with water and a sponge. If the joint compound is thick, dampen it with a wet sponge and gently remove the compound with a dull plastic trowel before sponging off the remainder.

MULTILAYER APPLICATIONS

Double or multiple layers of drywall are sometimes required for increased fire resistance or for decreased sound penetration. You can secure all layers with fasteners in the standard manner, but a good alternative is to use adhesive to attach the outermost, or "face," layer. Using adhesive increases the strength of the structure and reduces the number of fasteners needed. The use of drywall adhesives with single-layer applications was explained in Chapter 3; the procedure is the same when applying the face layer of drywall in multilayer applications. Apply a ⅜-in. bead of adhesive over the location of each framing member (see the top photo at right), and then fasten the panel around the perimeter and every 24 in. in the center of the panel.

You can also use joint compound as an adhesive to attach the face layer (see the bottom photo at right). Apply a strip of joint compound approximately ½ in. thick and 5 in. wide every 16 in. or 24 in. (depending on the framing spacing). Then use a notched trowel to groove the compound to leave beads of compound ⅜ in. wide by ½ in. high spaced 1 in. apart. When using this method for wall applications, prebow the panels (with the bow facing in against the wall) and fasten only the edges. For ceilings, you'll also need a fastener in the center of the panel on each framing member.

Apply a bead of adhesive at the location of the framing members when attaching the face layer of drywall in a multilayer application.

Joint compound can also be used as an adhesive when attaching the face layer of drywall.

Sound penetration through walls or ceilings can be a real problem in some homes and building complexes. Sound vibrations travel through the air and when they meet a wall or ceiling, the sound causes the surface to vibrate. For a wall, the vibration travels through the drywall into the framing and through the drywall on the other side. The vibration transmits the sound.

In order to reduce this type of sound penetration, walls or ceilings can be furred with a resilient channel, made of steel, which is screwed to the framing through an attachment flange. The channel floats the drywall away from the framing, thereby reducing the level of sound penetration caused by vibration. The channel should be attached perpendicular to the framing with screws (not nails) spaced 24 in. on center. For double-layer applications of drywall, I recommend 16-in. on-center spacing. The drywall is attached to the channel with the same type of fine-threaded screw used for attaching drywall to steel framing.

Resilient steel channel is also an excellent substitute for wood furring; it is usually less expensive, and the spring action of the resilient channel helps to level slightly uneven framing.

Resilient steel channel attached perpendicular to the framing is used to deaden sound and level ceilings. Fasten the drywall to the channel with fine-threaded screws.

When hanging drywall in two layers, attach the second layer of drywall perpendicular to the first layer so that seams don't align.

If you use screws or nails to attach double or multiple layers of drywall, it's important to attach each layer with the correct number of fasteners. *Never* just tack the first layer or layers and fasten only the last layer correctly. Each layer is heavy and must be attached properly to prevent sagging, loose panels and popped nails or screws. In addition, make sure that the screws for each layer penetrate the framing at least the minimum depth of ⅝ in. for wood and ⅜ in. for metal framing (see the chart on p. 29).

When installing double layers, it's best to attach the first layer parallel to the framing and the second layer across the framing. This layout will avoid having seams line up with each other that would provide openings for fire or sound to pass through. However, it's often easier to attach each layer perpendicular to the framing, especially if the on-center spacing of the framing is off. Just be careful to keep seams on the face layer away from seams on the underlying layer—panels should be staggered so that seams are at least 10 in. apart. On a ceiling, for example, start the first layer with a 24-in. wide panel and the second layer with a 48-in. wide panel. Use the longest lengths possible and make sure that any butted seams do not line up with butted seams on the first layer.

INSTALLING CEMENT BOARD

Cement board, which is used in areas exposed to high-water conditions (see p. 10), is cut with the score-and-snap method in much the same manner as drywall. Use a utility knife and a T-square or straightedge to cut through the glass mesh on one side. To break the panel at the cut, tap the back side with a hammer as you apply pressure away from the cut. Then cut the back side with a utility knife and snap forward again. The cement board will dull the utility knife very quickly, so change the blade often to ensure smooth and easy cuts. A carbide-tipped knife will keep a sharp edge a lot longer. You can also make square and round cutouts in cement board with a utility knife and a hammer (see the sidebar on the facing page).

Cement board should be attached with special galvanized nails or screws, not with drywall nails or screws. Galvanized nails used to attach metal roofing also work quite well (see the photo below). These nails have a large flat head and are ringed for added holding strength. Before attaching the cement board, it's a good idea to apply some construction adhesive to the studs. The adhesive adds strength to the structure, which is particularly important when tile is being applied over the cement board.

Galvanized metal-roofing nails are ideal for attaching cement board.

Straight cuts in cement board are made using the score-and-snap technique.

To cut a round opening in cement board, first mark the location of the opening on one side of the board. Drive a nail through the panel to help locate the opening on the back side. Cut through the fiberglass mesh with a utility knife, and then gently tap the opening on the finish side with a hammer until the cutout falls out. Chip away any irregular edges with the blade side of a drywall hammer.

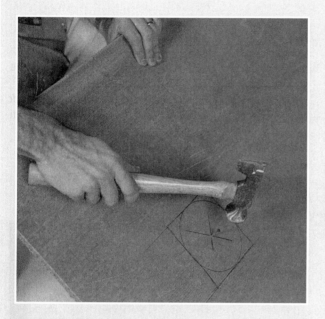

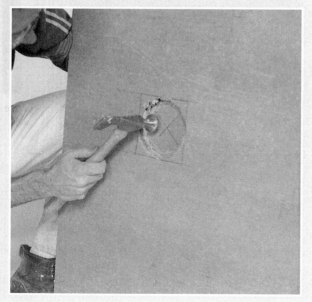

Mark the location of the opening on both sides of the panel, using a nail to locate the center of the opening on the back side (top left). Cut through the fiberglass mesh on both sides (above). Tap around the edges of the opening with a hammer until the cutout breaks apart and falls out (bottom left).

7
REPAIRS

No matter how good a job you do of hanging and taping drywall, there will inevitably come a time when you'll have to make some repairs. Drywall is not a rock-hard surface that can withstand repeated abuse, and some of the repairs are simply necessitated by the demands of day-to-day life in a busy household, where doorknobs may strike against the wall, pets may scratch and children may playfully bang their toys against anything in their path. Drywall does not add much structural strength to a building, and other repairs are required if the drywall develops cracks or ridges as a building settles. And remodeling often involves moving electrical outlets or light fixtures or closing off a window or doorway.

Repair of drywall, if done properly, is a permanent and inconspicuous part of the wall or ceiling surface. Some repairs are simple and can be done with one or two thin coats of joint compound, while others require additional framing and at least three coats of joint compound. The tools and taping techniques used for repair work are the same as those used for standard taping jobs.

POPPED NAILS AND SCREWS
Popped nails and screws are one of the most common drywall problems and the easiest to repair. They can occur when a drywall panel is not fastened tightly against the framing, when the framing lumber shrinks or twists, or when an object strikes the wall. The joint compound comes loose from the fastener and "pops off," exposing the fastener head or pushing out the joint tape. Fastener pops may appear soon after the wall or ceiling is finished, or it may take several years for them to show.

Whatever the cause of the pop, the best remedy is to remove or reset the fastener and then place another drywall screw about 1½ in. away. Apply hand pressure to the panel next to the area as you're setting the new screw. After the new screw or screws have been set, check the popped fastener and reset it again if necessary (or simply remove it).

If the paper surface of the drywall has not been damaged, the fasteners can be finished with three coats of joint compound and some light sanding. If the paper surface has been torn or the core of the drywall has been damaged, you should first apply a small piece of mesh tape to the damaged area.

Fastener depressions
A fastener depression is a recessed area around the fastener head where the joint compound is lower than the panel surface. The depression may have occurred because not enough joint compound was applied when taping; or the

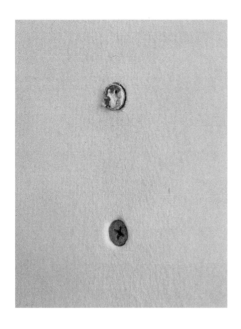

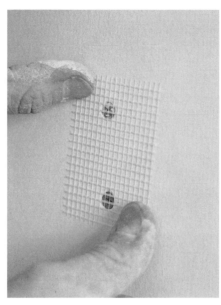

To repair a popped screw, place another screw 1½ in. away (far left) and then remove or reset the popped screw. If there is any damage to the drywall surface, cover the screws with mesh tape before applying the joint compound (left).

fastener may have been driven too deeply into the panel surface, damaging and weakening the panel's face paper and interior gypsum core. Fastener depressions often aren't visible until after you've painted.

In order to diagnose the problem, push firmly against the drywall panel next to the depression. If the panel is secure, you simply need to apply another coat or two of joint compound and then lightly resand to even out the depression. If the panel moves in and out even a slight amount, the panel is damaged. To correct the problem, place a screw 1½ in. away from the original fastener, and then press against the panel again to check for any movement. If the panel is now tight, remove any loose material from around the original fastener with a taping knife and then reset the nail or screw by tapping with a hammer or setting deeper with a screwdriver. Cut a piece of fiberglass-mesh tape to cover the fasteners, retape the area with three coats of joint compound and sand lightly when dry.

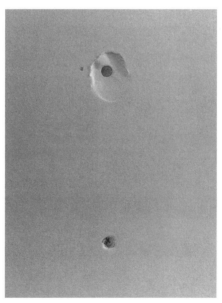

Both the nail and the screw shown here are set improperly, creating the potential for a depressed area around the fastener even after three coats of joint compound are applied.

To repair a fastener depression, place another fastener 1½ in. away, remove any loose material from around the original fastener and then reset the fastener.

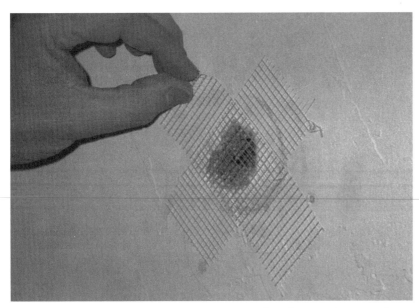

To repair a hole made by a doorknob or similar object, crisscross the hole with layers of mesh tape.

Force the joint compound into the mesh tape using a 6-in. taping knife, and then finish with two additional coats of compound.

REPAIRING HOLES IN DRYWALL

Holes in the drywall surface that result from long-term wear and tear range from small nail holes to large gouges. The extent of the repair needed depends on the size of the hole: Nail holes, nicks and small dents can just be covered with compound; small holes require paper or mesh for reinforcement; and larger holes require the use of furring strips to support the drywall patch.

Repairing small holes

A small nail hole (such as is left when a picture hung on the wall is repositioned) can usually be filled with just two or three coats of compound. Remove any loose material first and depress the area around the hole slightly with the handle of a utility knife.

Small holes or dents in drywall created when a blunt object such as a doorknob hits a wall can usually be repaired without having to cut out the damaged area and replace it with a piece of drywall. Completely cover the damaged area with mesh tape, crossing the tape over the hole, as shown in the top photo at left. (Depending on the size of the hole, you may be able to fill it with joint compound before applying the tape.) Next, apply joint compound over the tape with just enough trowel pressure to force the compound through the tape (see the photo on p. 110). Feather out the edges of the compound and do not build up the center too much (otherwise, you'll create a bump that will be visible in certain lighting). Apply the second and third coats, feathering out the area further and keeping the center thin.

Electrical outlet-box and switch covers usually don't cover an area much larger then the box itself, so it doesn't take much of a mistake when cutting out an opening for an electrical box before you have to do some patching.

Before starting the repair, make sure to turn off the power to the box. Then apply hand pressure against the drywall panel next to the box. If the panel seems loose, place a screw in the framing member closest to the box. (The patch will be stronger if the drywall is solidly screwed in place around the electrical box.)

Fill large gaps with joint compound first, and then cover the hole with mesh or paper tape and embed the tape in joint compound. When the joint compound is dry, apply a thin second coat that just covers the tape and blends it into the surrounding area. For a small patch, you usually need only two coats before sanding. If after sanding you think it still needs another coat, apply a thin coat and resand when dry.

An overcut electrical outlet box must be patched if the outlet plate will not cover the gap.

Fill the gap with joint compound.

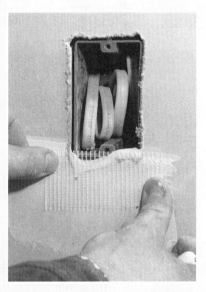

Cover the gap with a layer of mesh or paper tape.

Repairing large holes

If an area of drywall is badly damaged, the damaged area should be cut back to where the panel is solid. For ease of repair, make the opening square, rectangular or round (see the photos on p. 114). Once the damaged area is removed, the opening will probably be too large to repair with mesh tape and compound alone (as described on the facing page); you need something to attach the repair patch to. To provide a fastening surface for the patch, use a furring strip (or strips) cut about 6 in. longer than the hole. Slide the furring into the hole and hold it in place with drywall

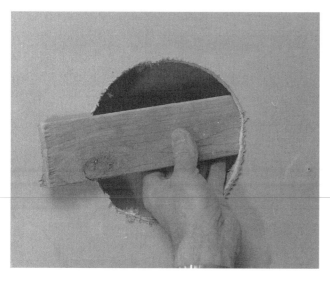

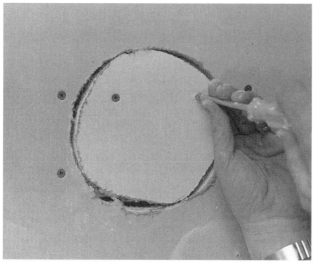

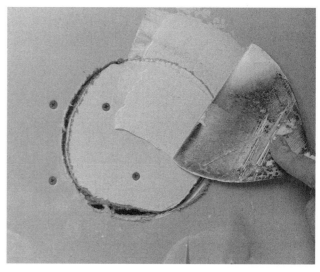

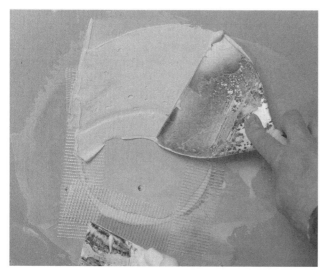

Use furring strips to provide a fastening surface for a large drywall patch (top left). Screw the furring strips into place on either side of the hole (top right). Screw the patch onto the furring (center left). Fill the gaps around the patch with joint compound (center right). Cover the edges of the patch with mesh tape and smooth with three coats of joint compound (bottom left).

To patch a disused electrical box, bevel the edges of the opening with a utility knife, and then cut the drywall patch to match.

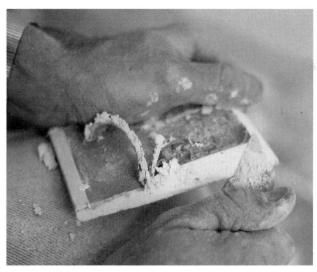

Bevel the back edges of the patch until it fits snugly into the hole without protruding past the face of the panel.

screws that go through the drywall panel and into the furring. Cut and shape the drywall patch to fit the hole, and then screw the patch onto the furring.

Now the patch can be taped. First, fill in any large gaps with joint compound, and then cover all the edges with fiberglass-mesh tape. Cover the tape with a thin layer of joint compound. Once again, be sure to feather out the edges properly and be careful not to build up the patched area too much. These larger holes will require at least three coats of joint compound to conceal properly. Since the patch has been secured to the panel and is now a solid part of the drywall, it is unlikely that the patch will crack or come loose.

For really large holes, furring strips won't be effective and you'll have to cut the drywall back to the nearest framing member and add cross-framing (as when eliminating a door or window; see pp. 116-118).

REMODELING REPAIRS

During remodeling work, electrical outlet boxes, heating ducts and other fixtures are often moved or eliminated, which means that the original hole has to be covered up and patched. You can install furring strips to support the patch, as described previously, but an alternative is to bevel the edges of the opening and the patch. When doors or windows are eliminated during remodeling, you'll need to add framing to the opening before patching with drywall.

Eliminating an electrical box

When an electrical box is eliminated, the box may be removed or left in the wall. If the box is still in place, make sure there are no electrical wires in the box (live electrical wires should be covered with a blank cover plate, not with drywall).

Start by trimming away any loose paper or drywall around the opening, and then bevel the outside edges with a utility knife. Next, cut a piece of drywall the same size as the opening (see the photo at left above), and bevel the back edges.

Apply joint compound around all edges of the patch.

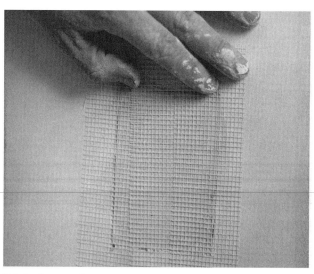

With the patch in place, cover the seams with mesh tape to prevent cracking, and then finish with three coats of joint compound.

Adjust the fit of the patch with a utility knife until the patch fits snugly into place without sticking out past the face of the drywall panel.

Apply a generous layer of joint compound to all edges of the patch (or the hole), and then press the patch into place, making sure it is flush with the panel surface. To prevent the patch from cracking along its edges, apply some fiberglass-mesh tape or paper tape to the seams and embed the tape in joint compound. Once the compound is dry, cover the tape with a second coat and feather the edges into the drywall face. Once the second coat is dry, lightly sand and apply a third coat if necessary.

Eliminating a door or window opening

For best results when eliminating a doorway or a window, you should ideally cover the entire wall with a new layer of drywall. However, it's not usually practical to re-drywall the whole wall, and the more common approach is to patch just the opening. A large patch such as a closed-off door or window opening has butted seams on all edges and is very difficult to hide unless great care is taken to do the job properly.

The first step is to frame in the opening (top left photo, facing page). Make sure that the framing lumber is straight, and install the framing so that it is held back a little from the back of the drywall already attached to the wall. (If the wall is finished with plaster, just frame in the opening so that a ½-in. thick piece of drywall will be flush or recessed slightly back from the finished wall surface.) Cut one piece of drywall to cover the opening. To avoid damaging the edges when screwing the patch in place, make sure the drywall doesn't fit too tightly (leave about ⅛ in. all around; top right photo, facing page). Fasten the drywall in place, and then cut away any high or loose edges with a utility knife or rasp.

Since the seams are all butted seams, I recommend using paper tape and a setting-type compound for the first coat for added strength (bottom left photo, facing page). Apply a wide second coat of compound, feathering out the edges.

When a window has been removed, frame in the opening with studs. Hold the studs back from the surface of the wall just a little more than the thickness of the drywall being used in the repair.

Fill in the opening with one piece of drywall, leaving about an ⅛-in. gap all around.

Treat all seams as butted seams, using paper tape and a setting-type joint compound.

Feather out the edges as you apply the second, third and fourth coats of compound.

Once the compound is dry, use a straightedge between coats to check for ridges and areas that need to be filled more. Usually four coats of joint compound are needed.

STRESS CRACKS

Stress cracks, which typically occur above a doorway or window, are caused by structural movement or settling. If a crack occurs where there is a seam, the tape may come loose and blister. A stress crack can also occur where there is no joint in the drywall: It may run along the panel face, or it may go all the way through to the other side.

To repair a stress crack, first cut out any loose drywall tape or joint compound with a utility knife or the corner of a taping knife. The V-groove formed provides a wider area for filling with joint compound. Next, apply hand pressure around the crack to check for movement. If the panel moves in and out, fasten it to the framing member closest to the crack. This will make the drywall more solid and less likely to crack again.

Fill any larger cracks with joint compound, and then cover the crack with mesh or paper tape. Smooth the area with two or three coats of compound and then sand. (In new construction, wait at least six months to a year, which is usually enough time for a structure to finish settling, before repairing stress cracks.)

WATER DAMAGE

Water damage to drywall is usually confined to the ceilings. A leaking roof and leaking plumbing in the upstairs bathroom are two common causes of water damage. What usually happens is that the water runs along the top of the drywall until it finds a seam or a corner. Once the joint compound on the seam or corner gets wet enough, the water will break through and run down the wall or onto the floor. The damage from this type of leak is usually not too extensive to the drywall itself, because the water found an exit and didn't lie on top of the drywall.

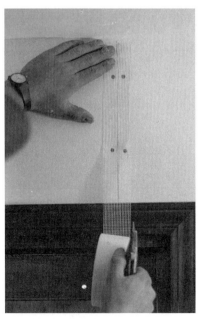

Cut along each side of the crack with a utility knife to form a V-groove (far left). If the drywall is loose around the crack, nail along the closest framing member, and then cover the crack with mesh tape (left).

To repair a water-stained ceiling, make sure that the damaged area is dry and then remove any loose material.

Roll on a coat of oil-based stain-killing paint over the stained area.

Once the stain-killing paint has dried, patch the damaged areas before repainting the entire ceiling.

Before repairing the drywall, first fix the roof or the plumbing to prevent further damage. Next, remove any loose tape and joint compound. If the drywall itself has come loose, allow it to dry out before attempting to refasten it. To prevent sagging, which would be difficult to correct when re-attaching the dried-out panel, prop the drywall up with a T-support or temporary furring strips. It's a good idea to go up into the attic and remove and dry out any insulation that may be wet. Removing the wet insulation will allow the drywall to dry out faster, and it may also prevent any further damage. When the drywall is thoroughly dry, it will return to its original strength and can be refastened. Any damage can be retaped using the same techniques that were described in Chapter 4.

If a section of drywall has bowed excessively between the ceiling joists because it has soaked up too much water, the affected area will have to be removed and the opening patched in the same way as a large hole.

Water stains

Along with water damage, you'll inevitably get some staining, and the stains will likely extend over a much larger area than the damage itself. Refasten or replace the damaged areas as described above, and then, before taping, seal all stained areas with a good-quality stain-killing paint. I prefer to use an oil-based rather than a latex stain killer because the stain is less likely to bleed through the joint compound.

Once the paint is thoroughly dry, patch the damaged and repaired areas, blending them into the ceiling surface. Before repainting, check the ceiling for any stains that may have bled through and reseal where necessary.

MILDEW DAMAGE

Under the right heat and humidity conditions, mildew can grow on any drywall surface. It usually occurs after the drywall has become wet.

To correct a mildew problem, you first have to eliminate the source of the moisture. If the problem occurs in a bathroom (the most common location), you may need to decrease the humidity in the room with an exhaust fan, a dehumidifier or a better supply of heat. Once the humidity problem has been corrected and the drywall has been allowed to dry out thoroughly, wash off the mildew stain with bleach and water (mixed roughly 1:2). Repair any damaged areas and re-paint with a mildew-resistant paint. Maintain the low-humidity conditions to prevent mildew from recurring.

8

DECORATING DRYWALL

Once all the drywall work is done, the final step is to decorate the drywall surfaces. Drywall can be finished with paint, texture finishes or wall coverings. In order to get satisfactory results, the finishing must be done properly—a poor finishing job can ruin even the most meticulous taping job.

PAINTING

Painting is a little more complicated than just buying some cheap primer and then rolling on a heavy coat of paint. The proper preparation before the final finish is applied will make an obvious difference.

Preparing for painting

The surface to be painted should be dry, clean, sound and free from oil or grease. Drywall manufacturers recommend that walls and ceilings should be dusted off before painting to remove the fine film of dust left from sanding, but in my experience there are no obvious benefits to this practice. I usually sand the walls lightly with fine sandpaper (200 grit works well) *after* the prime coat is dry. This light sanding removes any small chunks of paint or drywall, and it knocks down any raised fibers on the paper face of the drywall, leaving a very smooth surface.

Before painting, it is important to vacuum or dust out electrical boxes and to make sure that there is no dust above window or doorway trim. If you're working in a room with a finished floor, cover the floor with drop cloths to prevent damage from paint spattering; protect windows, doors, tubs, showers and other fixtures with 1-mil plastic (known in the trade as "painter's plastic").

The prime coat

It usually takes two coats of paint to finish drywall—one prime coat and one top coat. There's a confusing assortment of products on the market that are advertised as prime coats, and it's important to understand the difference between them.

"Primer" and "sealer" are commonly used to refer to the first coat of paint applied before the top coat, but these two terms do not refer to the same product. A primer is mainly made with fillers and pigments that are designed to equalize differences in surface textures and to provide a good base for the finish paint to bond to. Primers often do not contain enough resin to equalize the porosity of the different surfaces on the taped drywall; if they are used as the first coat over drywall, photographing of the seams and fasteners may be a problem (see the sidebar at top on the facing page).

The problem of photographing, whereby the taped seams and fasteners are visible through the painted surface in direct natural light, was mentioned in Chapter 4. Photographing is always a concern if a paint with a glossy finish (even an eggshell or a satin finish) is going to be used as the top coat. But even if you're going to finish the drywall with a latex flat paint, it's a good idea to prepare the surface to equalize the porosity and texture of the drywall surface and the taped seams. There are two ways to do this: by skim coating and by priming.

Skim coating the entire drywall surface after the third coat of joint compound has dried (see the sidebar on p. 82) is the best way to avoid the problem of photographing. Skim coating fills in any imperfections of the taping as it smooths the paper surface. After the skim coat is complete, a good quality primer-sealer or latex flat wall paint should be applied before finishing with the top coat.

Although effective, skim coating is time-consuming, and it is not a very widely used (or known) technique. (I've skim-coated only a dozen or so jobs over the years— I save it for small rooms, such as bathrooms that are going to be painted with a high-gloss paint, and highly visible jobs, such as large open ceilings that receive a lot of natural light.) A much more common technique is to prime all taped surfaces with a good-quality interior latex flat wall paint. Flat paints have a very low sheen because of the fillers used to formulate the paint, and these fillers help to equalize the differences between the drywall face paper and the taped seams and fasteners.

A sealer has a high resin content, which is good for equalizing the porosity of the taped surface, but it usually cannot correct differences in surface textures. Again, photographing may result after the top coat is applied. There is a product on the market called a primer-sealer that combines the qualities of both products. A good-quality primer-sealer does an adequate job as the prime coat, but it's not my first choice. I find that I get the best results when I prime with a good-quality interior latex flat wall paint.

Latex flat wall paint provides good coverage as a prime coat and minimizes the problem of photographing. If I'm working on walls that are going to be painted a color other than white, I usually have the flat latex paint tinted to the same color as the top coat to avoid having to apply two top coats.

After the drywall has been taped and sanded, don't let it sit too long before painting. Timely painting is especially important if the surface will be exposed to direct sunlight for any length of time. Sunlight can cause the face paper of the drywall to yellow or fade. If the face paper becomes too yellow, it may bleed through slightly when painted; the seams and fasteners will not bleed through, so the finish will look streaked. If the face paper has turned yellow, seal the drywall with a good-quality latex stain-killing paint before applying the latex flat prime coat.

The top coat

As with the prime coat, there's a bewildering array of paints that can be used as the top coat. These include flat, eggshell, satin, semi-gloss, gloss and high-gloss paints. Flat paints are less prone to photographing, but they are harder to maintain. Gloss paints (including eggshell and satin) are easier to wash than flat paints and are less likely to smudge and mark up; they are commonly used in bathrooms and kitchens and other areas that need frequent cleaning. Gloss paints are primarily wall paints. They are seldom used on ceilings because photographing, which is always a problem with gloss paints, is more pronounced on the large exposed surfaces of a ceiling.

Gloss paints are harder to apply than flat paints and may require two coats for a quality finish. Roller marks or lapped areas that have dried slightly before being blended in while painting are quite obvious on glossy painted surfaces. While flat paint can be applied as a prime coat, gloss paint should not be applied directly over a taped drywall surface. Always apply a prime coat first.

Painting techniques
There are three ways to apply paint to a wall or ceiling: with a brush, a roller or a sprayer. Paint brushes are used mainly for cutting in around trim and along inside corners. Rollers are used to fill in the large areas between the brushed-on edges. Sprayers, which are used to paint the entire surface, are primarily for large jobs in new construction.

Rollers are available in a variety of nap thicknesses for applying different types of paint and for achieving different texture finishes.

Rolling Paint rollers come in a variety of widths and nap thicknesses. A 9-in. wide roller, which is the most common size used, is excellent for small painting jobs and narrow sections of walls. Other roller widths are 12 in., 18 in. and 24 in. The larger-width rollers work well for bigger jobs, not only because they cover a larger area with each roller-full of paint, but also because they leave fewer roller marks, which would be more evident on a large, open surface.

The nap of a roller refers to the thickness of the fibers on the roller. Nap thicknesses range from 1/8 in. to 1/2 in. for regular painting; thicker naps are available for applying and painting texture finishes (see the photo below). For best results, gloss paints should be applied with a 1/4-in. nap (or thinner) roller. If the nap is too thick, small air bubbles will appear on the painted surface. These air bubbles soon pop, but they usually leave a small mark or thin spot on the paint surface that is still evident when the paint dries.

It's best to use a 3/8-in. nap roller for flat paints: A roller with a shorter nap does not cover the surface as well, and a longer nap leaves a slight texture on the surface. Longer-nap rollers (1/2-in. nap and up) are used for light texturing and for painting textured surfaces.

When painting with a roller, always apply the final coat by rolling on the paint across the direction of the taped seams. Each coat should be applied in the opposite direction to the one before it. For example, if two coats are being applied, the prime coat should be applied in the direction of the seams, and the final coat should be applied across the seams. By applying the final coat across the seams, the paint is applied more evenly and there is less chance of any spots being missed. The roller will flow over any minor ridges or crowns along the seams, covering them with paint.

When painting with a roller, apply the prime coat in the direction of the taped seams and the top coat across the seams.

Spraying If you use a sprayer to apply the paint, I recommend a paint sprayer that applies the paint undiluted, like the one shown in the photos on p. 124. The paint is pumped directly from a 1-gal. or 5-gal. pail, and applied with a hand-held spray gun that is fed through a hose.

When using a paint sprayer, there is a certain amount of overspray and some airborne paint, so a respirator or dust/mist mask should be worn. You'll also need to mask off walls and other areas that you don't want to get paint on.

When using a paint sprayer, wear a respirator and cover walls and other surfaces as necessary to protect them from overspray.

To achieve a smooth, even finish and save time, apply the paint with a sprayer and then roll it out.

When spraying paint, follow the same procedure used when painting with a roller. Start by applying a prime coat, and then follow with the top coat. It may be tempting to spray on a good heavy coat of paint and be done, but the paint would just run or drip. For best results, apply thin even coats (usually one prime and one top coat for flat paints, one prime and two top coats for gloss).

Spraying paint is much faster than rolling paint, mainly because the paint is always right at the paint nozzle. With

most rollers, the roller has to be dipped into the roller pan repeatedly (although there are now rollers with automatic feed). For finish painting, I prefer the look of a finish that has been rolled on—it just seems to be more uniform and consistent. In order to achieve both the speed of the sprayer and the finish of a roller, the paint can be applied with a sprayer and then rolled out into a smooth, even finish by a helper following close behind the person with the sprayer (see the photo at right above).

TEXTURING

Decorating ceilings and walls with a textured finish is a very popular alternative to painting. Textured finishes, which can be produced in a wide variety of patterns, add beauty and contrast to drywalled surfaces, are excellent at hiding minor surface imperfections and irregularities and, in their coarser forms, provide a certain degree of sound control. Most of my work is done with sprayed-on textures, although I do occasionally apply texture by hand (see pp. 130-131). The textures I use are easy to apply, quick-drying and odor-free.

Preparing for texturing

Using textures reduces the amount of surface preparation required, but the surface must still be clean, dry and sound. Textured finishes are only as good as the surfaces they are applied to. Always apply a prime coat to new drywall and to any area where repairs have been made. If the surface is not new but has a clean, flat, painted surface, no prime coat is necessary.

Seal any stains with an oil-based stain-killing paint. Apply texture to a small test area to check for any stain bleed-through. Most textures are high in water content and take about 24 hours to dry. If a stain is not properly sealed, the stain will quickly bleed through and discolor the texture.

Ceilings that have yellowed as a result of years of exposure to cigarette smoke need special preparation before they are textured over. The surfaces should be washed before any necessary repairs are made and then primed with a latex flat wall paint. As an extra precaution, texture a small test area to check for stain bleed-through. If the texture in the test area is still white after an hour or so, then it should be safe to texture the entire surface.

Water-based textures may cause drywall on a ceiling to sag between joists if the maximum on-center spacing of joists for the thickness of the drywall is exceeded (see Chapter 1). Three-eighth-inch drywall is not recommended on ceilings, especially if the ceiling is going to be textured. If you're texturing over $\frac{1}{2}$-in. drywall, the spacing of the joists should not exceed 16 in. on center; for $\frac{5}{8}$-in. drywall, the spacing can be up to 24-in. on center. For both thicknesses, the drywall should be attached perpendicular to the joists.

The air surface and texture temperature should be at least 55°F during and after application of a texture. Once the texture has been applied, the room should be properly ventilated to help the texture dry. In an unventilated room, the risk of

GENERAL GUIDELINES FOR TEXTURING

- Make sure the surface is clean. Seal any stains and texture a test area to check for bleed-through.

- Fill any cracks or holes in the surface and tape to a smooth finish.

- Allow taped areas to dry completely before texturing.

- Use a latex flat wall paint as a prime coat so the surface to be textured has a flat finish.

- Maintain a temperature of at least 55°F before, during and after the texture is applied. Keep the area well ventilated while the texture is drying.

- For ceiling textures, make sure the on-center spacing of the joists meets maximum recommended guidelines in order to avoid potential sagging problems.

- Cover areas that are not going to be textured or clean up overspray promptly.

- Dull or roughen any glossy surfaces for better adhesion of the prime coat.

In new construction, any overspray from the ceiling can be scraped off the walls with a wide trowel and, when dry, sanded before the walls are decorated. If a wall texture is going to be applied, very little sanding is necessary.

If the walls are already sanded or decorated, they will have to be protected from the overspray.

I like to use a 12-in. wide strip of paper masked around the edge of the ceiling. A tool that applies the tape to the paper edge as the paper is unrolled works great for this purpose. The paper machine and paper can be purchased at any auto-body supply store.

A certain amount of texture settles to the floors and lower walls as the ceiling is sprayed. Protect floors with drop cloths and walls with 1-mil painter's plastic. Tuck and tape the plastic up and underneath the 12-in. wide paper along the ceiling. Taking the time to cover everything before texturing makes for quick and easy cleanup at the end of the job.

To protect walls and light fixtures from overspray use a 12-in. wide strip of paper with masking tape (top left). A paper roller machine is available that applies the tape to the paper as the paper is unrolled (above). Cover floors with drop cloths and walls with painter's plastic (bottom left).

the drywall sagging is increased as the moisture is absorbed into the drywall panels. Under very hot and dry conditions, the texture may dry too quickly causing cracking and a poor bond.

Textures are usually applied with special spray equipment. For residential work, textures are most commonly sprayed on with a hand-held hopper (see the photo at right below) and an air compressor. For commercial work, larger texturing machines that feed the texture through a hose into a spray gun are used. Spray equipment can be rented.

Sprayed-on acoustical ceiling textures

Sprayed-on acoustical textures, often referred to as popcorn ceilings, are one of the most common and easiest to apply textures. The texture comes in a dry form that contains different-size solid particles that determine the coarseness of the texture and are mixed with water to the recommended consistency. The solid particles in the texture are made of either vermiculite (puffed mica) or polystyrene. The texture grades are coarse, medium and fine. The appearance of each grade can be varied by how densely the texture is applied; instructions for heavier applications are listed on the bag. To achieve the desired

Use a hand-held hopper to apply a popcorn-ceiling texture.

Popcorn-ceiling textures are available in coarse (shown here), medium and fine grades.

heavy texture, two coats may be necessary. Apply the second coat of texture after the first coat is thoroughly dry.

After mixing the dry texture with the recommended amount of water, use a hand-held hopper or spray gun to apply the texture. Spray the texture by holding the applicator 2 ft. to 4 ft. away from the surface (see the photo at right on p. 127). Move the sprayer from side to side as you walk around the room and apply a thin even layer. Then double back and apply another layer going around the room in the opposite direction. Working this way will help you avoid any signs of a pattern or streaks that could result if the texture were applied from a single direction. Finish the entire ceiling in one session—if you stop in the middle, a noticeable edge will be visible where the texture has dried.

For an interesting decorative effect, popcorn ceilings are sometimes sprinkled with glitter. The glitter is blown onto the ceiling when the texture is still wet. Glitter comes in a wide variety of colors and sparkles as it reflects light.

Painting and repairing a popcorn ceiling It is not usually necessary to paint popcorn ceilings since the texture is white and will stay white unless exposed to smoke from cigarettes, kerosene heaters or fireplaces. However, popcorn ceilings can be painted if a more durable and easier-to-clean surface is required (an unpainted popcorn ceiling is not washable) or if a different color is desired. It may also be necessary to paint over the texture if it is stained or discolored for any reason.

Use a sprayer to apply latex paint to a popcorn ceiling; latex paint is water based and will loosen the texture and damage the ceiling if rolled on. If you want to paint the ceiling with a roller, use a flat oil-based paint with a long-nap roller (½ in. thick or thicker). Wait 24 hours for a freshly textured popcorn ceiling to dry before painting. If you want to use glitter, it can be blown onto the wet paint as the paint is applied.

If a popcorn ceiling is damaged or badly stained, and it is determined that the best way to fix the ceiling is to retexture (rather than just repaint), scrape off the entire ceiling with a wide taping knife. Repair the affected area, reprime, and then spray on a new layer of texture. If the majority of the ceiling is still nice and white, damaged areas can be repaired and then resprayed. Scrape the texture off with a taping knife and feather the edges of the removed area into the remaining texture to avoid any ridged edges that might show when the ceiling is retextured. To repair cracks in textured ceilings, scrape off the texture around the crack, patch the crack and then prime and retexture. Small damaged areas can be touched up by mixing a small amount of texture and applying it to the area with a paint brush.

Sprayed-on wall textures

Wall textures add a beautiful effect to the surface, but because a wall is exposed to more wear and tear, the texture has to be durable and easy to wash and paint. Two very popular wall textures (which also make excellent ceiling textures) are orange-peel texture and knock-down texture. Each texture is applied with the same spraying equipment that is used to spray on popcorn ceilings. The size of the nozzle opening and the air pressure are adjusted to achieve the desired pattern.

You can buy special texturing compounds to create these textures, but I find that I can get excellent results using an all-purpose joint compound that has been watered down and mixed thoroughly. (Setting-type compounds are not recommended because they can set up in the spraying equipment and removal would be very difficult.)

To create an orange-peel texture, spray thinned-down joint compound onto the wall with a hand-held hopper.

The look of the orange-peel design can be varied by adjusting the air pressure of the compressor and the diameter of the spray nozzle.

Orange-peel texture An orange-peel texture is achieved by thinning down the joint compound with water so that it will flow easily through the spraying equipment yet once applied will stay in place without running or sagging. Apply a test area before finishing the entire surface. Hold the spray nozzle at a consistent distance from the wall, approximately 2 ft. to 3 ft. away, and apply the texture evenly. Keep the texture consistent by mixing all the joint compound to the same thickness and setting the airflow and nozzle opening the same throughout the job.

Knock-down texture To create a knock-down texture, apply the joint compound just the same as for an orange-peel texture. Wait about 10 minutes, and then use a large flat trowel with a curved blade to knock down the raised surface of the orange-peel texture (see the top left photo on p. 130). Pull the trowel lightly along the surface, holding the blade almost flat and applying very little pressure. For best results pull the trowel across the seams.

The size of the spatter areas for the orange-peel and knock-down textures can be varied by adjusting the amount of pressure used in the spray gun, the size of the hole in the spray nozzle or the thickness of the joint-compound mixture. Both the orange-peel and knock-down textures can be applied directly over a freshly taped drywall surface. If used in redecorating, the surface should be smooth and solid, and should

Use a large flat trowel with a curved blade over a sprayed-on orange-peel texture to create a knock-down texture.

A knock-down texture applied over drywall is easy to paint and maintain.

The left side of this photo shows a roller texture. The right side shows the roller texture after it has been knocked down with a wide, flat trowel.

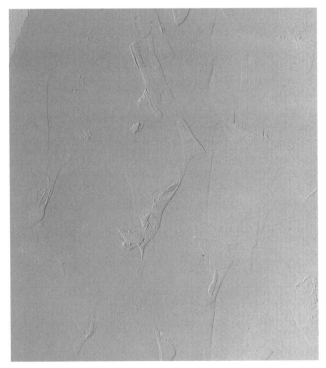

A hand-trowel finish is created by applying undiluted joint compound with a taping tool.

be painted with a latex flat wall paint before texturing. If the surface is irregular and wavy, a knock-down texture is not recommended because the trowel would just hit the high areas and leave the low areas untouched, resulting in a spotty appearance. Once orange-peel and knock-down textures are dry, they should be painted so that the surface will be washable and more durable.

Hand-applied textures

In addition to the sprayed-on textures, there are also many textures that can be applied by hand. Some of these textures have patterns that repeat, which require a very steady hand to perfect. I have better luck with hand-applied textures that have a nice, even, uniform finish or intentional irregularities. The textures discussed here, which can be created with texturing compound, all-purpose compound and even setting-type compound, are all simple to apply and easy to maintain.

Roller texture Water down the joint compound to a consistency that will hold its shape when rolled onto the drywall surface and not run or sag. Use a short-nap roller (½ in. thick or less) and apply the compound as evenly as possible to the entire surface. Let the compound dry for 10 minutes or so until the surface looks dull. Now go over the surface with the roller again, leaving the desired textured look.

Knock-down roller finish To achieve the knock-down roller finish, follow the same procedure as for the roller texture. After the roller texture is applied, wait a few minutes and then use the large flat trowel with the curved blade to flatten the texture. Hold the trowel almost flat against the surface and use very little pressure as you pull it along in the same direction that the roller was used to create the texture.

Hand-trowel finish To achieve the hand-trowel finish, I use undiluted joint compound. Apply a thin layer of compound to the entire surface in an irregular, random design using a 6-in. taping knife. The thickness of the compound will vary from some areas that are bare to areas that are ⅛ in. or so thick. Trowel marks, ridges and low areas are desirable when creating this finish.

Once dry, all these hand-applied textures should be decorated with a good-quality paint for easy maintenance and a more durable finish. Usually one coat of paint is sufficient to cover the surface.

PREPARING DRYWALL FOR WALL COVERINGS

Drywall is an excellent surface for all types of wall coverings, including regular wallpaper, fabric-backed wallpaper and vinyl-paper-backed cloth. The surface being covered with wallpaper should be sound, as smooth as possible, and free of peeling paint or plaster. If the surface is rough and loose, the wall covering will also be rough and loose and will not adhere securely. Thinner, shinier coverings require a smoother finished wall because they hide very few blemishes. Heavier wall coverings do not require nearly as perfect a finish. Also keep in mind that, as with textures, wall coverings are applied wet, so it is important that stains be sealed properly so that the moisture from the wall covering's adhesive will not cause the stain to bleed through.

For most wall coverings, the drywall should be taped with three coats of joint compound and then sanded smooth. Then a coat of latex flat wall paint should be applied. Once the paint is completely dry, a good-quality primer-sizer should be applied over the prime coat before the application of the wall covering can begin.

INDEX

PUBLISHER: Jon Miller

ACQUISITIONS EDITOR: Julie Trelstad

EDITORIAL ASSISTANT: Karen Liljedahl

EDITOR: Peter Chapman

PRODUCTION EDITOR: Diane Sinitsky

DESIGNER: Henry Roth

PHOTOGRAPHER: Jay Holz

ILLUSTRATOR: Scott Bricher

TYPEFACE: Frutiger Light

PAPER: Finch Opaque, 70 lb.

PRINTER: Quebecor Printing/Hawkins, New Canton, Tennessee